shortcuts to success

italian cooking

Ursula Ferrigno

photography by Peter Cassidy

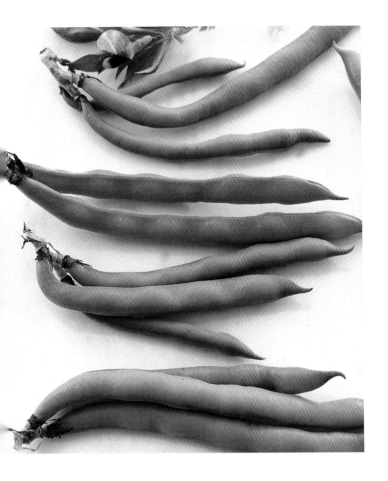

First published in the UK in 2003 by Quadrille Publishing Limited
Alhambra House 27-31, Charing Cross Road, London WC2H OLS

This edition published by Silverback Books, Inc., San Francisco, California. www.silverbackbooks.com

Editorial director Jane O'Shea **Creative director** Helen Lewis
Managing editor Janet Illsley **Art direction and design** Vanessa Courtier
Photographer Peter Cassidy **Food stylist** Linda Tubby **Props stylist** Jane Campsie
Editor Susan Fleming **Production** Vincent Smith and Jane Rogers

Text © 2003 Ursula Ferrigno Photography © 2003 Peter Cassidy
Design and layout © 2003 Quadrille Publishing Limited

Cataloging in Publication Data: a catalog record for this book is available from the British Library.

ISBN 1-930603-14-2
Printed in China

contents

Notes
Measurements are in standard American cups and spoons.

Use fresh herbs unless dried herbs are suggested.

Use freshly ground black pepper unless otherwise stated.

Eggs from cage-free or free-range hens are recommended, and extra large eggs should be used except where a different size is specified.

Recipes that feature raw or lightly cooked eggs should be avoided by vulnerable people (anyone who is pregnant, babies and young children, the elderly, and those who are sick or have compromised immune systems), unless using eggs pasteurized in shell.

introduction

Italian cuisine is arguably the most delectable, the most influential, and the best-loved cuisine in the world. Italian recipes have made an enormous difference to the way we cook. Quite apart from the perpetual presence of the best-known Italian exports in our lives—pasta, pizza, and Parmesan cheese, to name a few—so many things we eat have their roots in Italian cuisine. The way we assemble a salad, prepare a pasta dish, or grill a piece of fish or meat all indicate how strong these influences are. When the preparation of food is at its simplest and best, more often than not it owes a debt to the Italian kitchen.

That Italian cooking is so simple virtually guarantees success every time you start to work in the kitchen. I truly believe that the essence of good food lies in its simplicity, and endorse the popular Italian saying "*piu se spenne peggio se magna*" ("the more you spend, the less well you eat"). Italian food is not expensive or difficult: it's all about good basic ingredients, simply prepared and lovingly cooked, to produce a totally memorable meal that hasn't taken all day to create. When you come home from work tired and hungry, there is nothing simpler than a bruschetta with an interesting topping (possibly one that is already in the pantry), or a plate of pasta served with a fast sauce (see pages 86–7).

There are no difficult techniques to master in Italian cooking, although pastamaking and breadmaking are more time-consuming and a little more complex. Both lie at the heart of the Italian eating experience and, once you have learned the simple rules, you will be able to create fabulous breads, pizzas, and homemade pasta. I love making breads, and think of the live dough in its bowl as a friend in the kitchen, something that is growing, something to be nurtured, until it is ready to be made into a delectable bread, or indeed pizza. Because Italian cooking is essentially easy, it inspires confidence in the kitchen. And a confident cook, working with good ingredients, is a successful cook.

All the recipes here are easily achievable. All are authentically Italian—even those I've invented myself have their roots firmly in Italian tradition. Having been brought up in Italy, and having learned the huge respect accorded to food and eating at first hand, my recipes could be nothing other than traditional. The book is roughly arranged as an Italian meal would be, beginning with easy antipasti or appetizers, soups, and breads. The course that follows—pasta, polenta, or risotto—is also simple. Neither of these courses needs to be large in volume, because there are still three more to follow: meat or seafood, vegetables, and dessert. But if this meal structure sounds daunting, it need not be. Many Italians eat only a "full meal" on special occasions, or on the weekend, when there is more time to cook—and more time to talk, argue, laugh, savor, and enjoy.

Enjoyment is the most characteristic aspect of Italian cooking and eating, and I hope that the recipes here will persuade you into the kitchen, that they will enhance your life, and give you endless pleasure.

the Italian pantry

The essence of Italian cooking, apart from its simplicity, is its freshness—meat or fish, vegetables, and fruit are bought daily in Italy, and are chosen according to the season. But there are certain essentials that will be kept in the pantry, or *la dispensa,* and renewed regularly when needed. The Italian pantry—indeed anyone's pantry—should be stocked so that the basics for a delicious meal are always at hand.

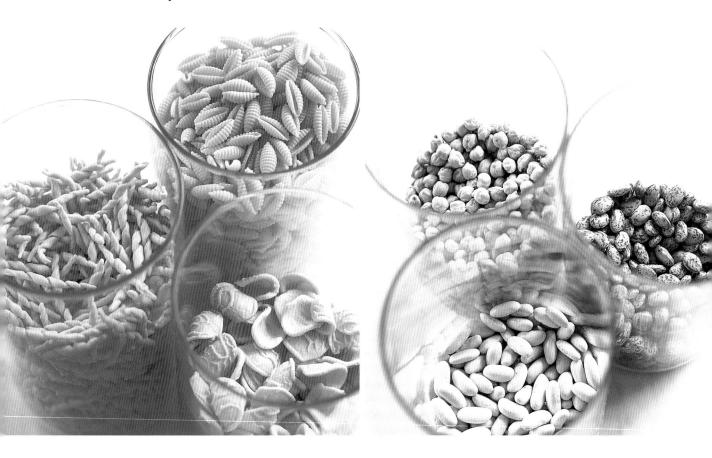

Pasta

Perhaps surprisingly, Italians tend to eat more dried pasta than fresh. Pasta is made at home, but usually only for special occasions. For the daily pasta course, the choice would normally be dried. I suggest you keep a selection of different types in your pantry: long pasta, such as tagliatelle and spaghetti; short pasta such as macaroni, conchiglie, farfalle, and fusilli; and pastina or very small pasta shapes.

Choose the variety of pasta according to the sauce you intend to serve. Long ribbon pastas of varying thicknesses, such as tagliatelle, are best served with butter, tomato, cream, and fish sauces. Spaghetti and linguine are matched by pesto, tomato, fish, and meat sauces, including Bolognese of course. Short pasta shapes, such as orecchiette and conchiglie, are best with vegetable sauces, the curves and indentations of the pasta ideal for holding small morsels of sauce. And the tiny shapes of pastina—from stellini to farfalline—are destined for soups.

Rice and grains

Italy relies on many grains, but the most important is wheat, which is made into flours for bread and pasta. Wheat flours come in a number of forms, graded by their fineness and suitability for different types of cooking. The best Italian pantry would contain farina "00," or *doppio zero,* for making fresh pasta, pastry, and cakes; "0" grade for pizza; and semolino duro, a ground durum wheat flour used in the making of commercial pasta and gnocchi. There would also be unbleached bread flour for breadmaking, flour for pastry, and self-rising flour for cakes. Farro is an ancient type of wheat also known as spelt. It is now enjoying a resurgence in popularity, and is being cultivated for use mainly in soups, like my farro and bean soup (page 51).

Rice, grown in the valley of the Po river and its tributaries in the north of Italy, is another staple. Risotto is the most famous of Italy's rice dishes and there are three main varieties of risotto rice for making it— arborio, carnaroli, and vialone nano. The principal characteristic of risotto rice is its ability to absorb moisture, thus enlarging the grain. The grain softens and develops a creamy texture, while retaining a bite, described as *al dente* (to the tooth). Rice is also used in soups, snacks, salads, stuffings, and as a main course accompaniment.

The third most important grain for the pantry is polenta. This is a yellow or white cornmeal. A staple in northern Italy, polenta is available in two forms. The one I prefer is the standard coarse grain, which needs up to 40 minutes to cook. The other is a quick-cook polenta, which may not be quite as tasty, but is perfectly acceptable when enriched with butter and cheese. Polenta can be served "wet," straight from the pan, as an accompaniment to a meat, mushroom, or vegetable stew or sauce. Or, it can be left until cold and set, then sliced and served instead of bread. The slices may also be fried or grilled to accompany meats, poultry or game birds, and sausages. Sometimes set polenta is enriched with butter, cheese, and other flavorings.

Legumes

When in season, shell beans are eaten fresh in Italy; at other times of the year they are used dried— no Italian pantry would be without packages of dried cannellini or borlotti (cranberry) beans, chick peas (garbanzo beans), or Castelluccio lentils. With these, you will never be short of something to cook that will be nutritious and satisfying. Most legumes require long soaking to rehydrate them, and then take quite a time to cook. If you are in a hurry, canned beans are a good alternative and make useful standby items for the pantry.

Nuts and seeds

These need to be bought fresh and used fairly regularly because they contain oils that can turn rancid. (Storing them in the fridge or freezer helps prolong their life.) Walnuts, hazelnuts, almonds, and pine nuts are used extensively in Italian cooking, in both sweet and savory dishes. Seeds, such as fennel, anise, and sesame, make wonderful flavorings and garnishes, and they are highly nutritious.

Dried fruit

Keep a selection of plump, moist dried apricots, prunes, figs, and raisins in your pantry to use for breads, desserts, and sweets. If possible, choose dried fruit that has not been treated with sulfur dioxide.

Oils and butter

Olive oil is the bottled essence of Italy. It is used extensively everywhere now, particularly since the virtues of the so-called "Mediterranean diet" and its almost exclusive use of olive oil became known. Oils are graded according to acidity—extra virgin olive oil has the lowest acidity, is the purest and most flavorful. Thrifty housekeepers—whether from Umbria, Puglia, Tuscany, or Liguria—will always have a bottle or two of the local new season's oil (available from November usually), which they will use only for dressings and as a condiment—sprinkled generously over a thick soup, for instance.

Extra virgin olive oil is best reserved for dressings. It is not used in cooking, as heat damages the proteins. Virgin olive oil is usually produced from more mature olives, is higher in acidity, and can be used for light cooking or in dressings such as mayonnaise. Straightforward olive oil is what you should use for cooking. This is also the oil to utilize for preserving vegetables or making a flavored oil. I like to do this at Christmastime: olive oil in a nice bottle, with floating herbs and chili peppers, makes a good present for friends and family.

Unsalted butter is another Italian cooking medium, used mainly in the north, although it features in cake- and cookie-making throughout the rest of the country.

Cheeses

The most vital cheese in the Italian pantry is Parmesan, as it has so many uses. It is perishable and should therefore be kept in the fridge, but it has a good shelf life. Keep a piece ready for grating, well wrapped to prevent it from drying out, in the vegetable keeper of the fridge. To use at its best, buy little and often.

Vinegars

A selection of vinegars will feature in any Italian pantry. Red and white wine vinegars are both used in cooking and salad dressings, but the most highly prized vinegar in Italy is balsamic, or *aceto balsamico*. This is probably the most expensive condiment in the Italian kitchen, because the maturation process is so lengthy and involved, but a drop or two of an aged balsamic can transform a dish. The finest balsamic vinegars, labeled *aceto balsamico tradizionale di Modena*, are over 30 years old, but you can buy less expensive and still exceptionally good balsamic vinegar aged from 5 to 20 years (similarly labeled but missing the word *tradizionale*).

Basic flavorings

The primary flavoring spices of any kitchen, including the Italian one, are salt, pepper, and sugar. I always use sea salt (coarse and flake varieties, and fine table salt), and grind my pepper freshly from black peppercorns. Of the sugars, I keep superfine, granulated, brown, and confectioners'. I also store a vanilla bean in a container of granulated sugar, so I always have some fragrant vanilla sugar to hand.

Herbs, spices, and aromatics

Most Italian housekeepers would have fresh herbs almost constantly to hand in pots on the windowsill or in the garden—basil, flat-leaf parsley, marjoram, thyme, sage, and mint in particular. However, dried oregano is an essential pantry item, and one of the few herbs that is actually improved by drying. If you have oregano in the garden, you can dry small bunches, if you like. Dried bay leaves are also worth

stocking, and you can dry these if you have a bay tree in the garden. Garlic is, of course, a vital flavoring in many Italian dishes, so you will need to keep a supply of fresh garlic bulbs.

Dried chili peppers are very popular in southern Italy, and small, fiery red chilies, called peperoncini, appear in a variety of dishes. These should be used cautiously as they are very hot.

The other spices most commonly encountered are nutmeg, juniper berries, paprika, cinnamon, cloves, and saffron. Keep whole nutmeg and grate freshly as required. Ground spices should be bought in small quantities, as they lose flavor during lengthy storage. Saffron is best bought as threads as these are less liable to be adulterated than the powdered alternative. This revered and expensive spice is used for a classic risotto milanese. Vanilla beans and vanilla extract lend an inimitable flavor to many Italian desserts and ice creams.

Dried mushrooms

These are a primary source of flavor in the Italian kitchen and a package or two of dried porcini is essential in the pantry. Fresh wild mushrooms are collected and eaten enthusiastically all over Italy in the autumn, but at other times of year, they are used dried—and lend extraordinary flavor to many dishes. Rehydrate by soaking in warm water to cover for about 20 minutes (strain and save the water for stock, as it will be full of flavor).

Other pantry essentials

There are so many important pantry items in an Italian kitchen, it is hard to name them all. The tomato, which is essential in so many Italian dishes, will be on the shelves in various guises. Canned plum tomatoes, whole or crushed (often with added herbs), sit alongside "passata" (cooked puréed tomatoes), sun-dried tomatoes, and, perhaps, sun-dried tomato paste.

Artichokes are preserved in oil, capers are brined or salted, and anchovies are salted or preserved in oil. (The salt from capers and anchovies must be rinsed off before use.) Olives are preserved in brine or oil, often with other flavorings; my favourite is the Gaeta olive. Truffles flavor oils or are condensed with porcini to make an expensive, but delicious, paste. A can or two of tuna, in brine or oil, can be used in a matter of moments to make a salad or sauce.

On the sweet side, I like to have jars of apricot jam and honey available—good on breakfast toast, or in baking and desserts. I'm not a chocoholic, but some good bittersweet chocolate is great in desserts, as is cocoa powder. Even the coffee beans so vital for the espresso can be used in cooking. And I always keep amaretti cookies, to serve with coffee, use in my dessert recipes, or crumble over ice cream.

The Italian pantry should also boast a limited selection of alcohol. Red and white wines, vermouth, Marsala and Vin Santo, and spirits such as brandy and the uniquely Italian grappa, add flavor and character to many sauces and desserts.

1 antipasti

warm seafood salad

Insalata calla di mare is a very popular antipasto, and every region of Italy has its own version. You can vary the fish, but do include a variety of textures, avoiding oily fish, as the flavor would be too pronounced. This salad is best served warm.

SERVES 6

1 lb fresh mussels

2 tablespoons dry white wine

1 dried hot chili pepper

1 lb squid, cleaned

2 tablespoons white wine vinegar

1 onion, peeled and halved

2 bay leaves

1 lb monkfish fillet, skinned

6 sea scallops

12 large, raw shrimp in shell

sea salt and freshly ground black pepper

handful of black olives

FOR THE DRESSING:

1 garlic clove, peeled and crushed

handful of flat-leaf parsley, minced

3 tablespoons lemon juice

3 tablespoons virgin olive oil

1 Discard any broken mussels, and those that do not close when sharply tapped. Scrub the mussels thoroughly in cold water and pull out the "beards," if any, then place in a large saucepan with the wine. Cover and cook over a high heat for about 4 minutes until they open, shaking the pan occasionally. Lift out the mussels with a slotted spoon, discarding any that remain closed. When cool enough to handle, shell the mussels and place in a bowl. Pour the cooking liquid through a cheesecloth-lined strainer onto the mussels. Add the dried chili pepper, stir, and set aside.

2 Rinse the squid well and cut the pouches into ½-inch rings, keeping the tentacles whole (if available). Put 6 cups of water into a saucepan with 1 tablespoon of the vinegar, the onion, 1 bay leaf, and some salt, and bring to a boil. Add the squid and cook at a steady simmer until opaque and you can pierce them with a fork, about 5 minutes depending on size. Remove with a slotted spoon, drain well, and add to the mussels.

3 Cut the monkfish into large chunks and add to the water in which the squid was cooked. Simmer gently for about 2 minutes. Remove from the heat, leaving the fish in the liquid.

4 Meanwhile, heat 1¼ cups water in another pan with the remaining bay leaf and vinegar, and some salt. When it comes to a boil, add the scallops and simmer gently for 2 minutes. Remove with a slotted spoon and set aside with the mussels and squid. Add the shrimp to the scallop cooking water, bring to a simmer, and cook for 1 minute. Drain and, when cool enough to handle, peel, leaving the tail on if you like. Drain the monkfish and add to the other seafood along with the shrimp. Remove and discard the chili pepper.

5 For the dressing, combine the garlic, parsley, and lemon juice in a small bowl. Add a generous grind of black pepper and some salt. Whisk in the olive oil, then taste and adjust the seasoning. Toss the seafood with the dressing and divide among shallow bowls. Serve immediately, while still warm, with the olives scattered over.

stuffed mussels

A really tasty classic from Campania, the region where I was brought up, this can be served with a wedge of lemon for a simple antipasto. The mussels are cooked to open, then topped in their half shell with a stuffing of garlic, parsle,y and bread crumbs, and baked briefly. The stuffing is a basic recipe to which other ingredients, such as tomato sauce and capers, can be added.

SERVES 4

2¼ lb mussels
2 lemons, cut into quarters
4 garlic cloves, peeled
3 tablespoons dry white wine
4 tablespoons olive oil
large handful of flat-leaf parsley,
  minced
2½ cups fresh white bread crumbs
  (slightly dry)
sea salt and freshly ground black pepper
lemon wedges for serving

1 Preheat the oven to 425°F. Discard any broken mussels, and those that do not close when sharply tapped. Scrub the mussels thoroughly in cold water and pull out the little "beards," if any.

2 Put the lemon quarters, garlic, and white wine into a large sauté pan or wide saucepan. Add the mussels, cover with a tight-fitting lid, and cook over a high heat for 5 minutes until the shells open, shaking the pan occasionally. Discard any mussels that remain closed.

3 Using a slotted spoon, remove the mussels from the pan, reserving the liquid. Remove and discard the empty half shells. Loosen the mussels in the bottom shells and place the shells on a baking sheet.

4 Filter the reserved cooking liquid through a cheesecloth-lined strainer into a bowl. Mix in the olive oil, parsley, bread crumbs, and salt and pepper to taste. Spoon a little of the mixture over each mussel. Bake for about 7 minutes until the topping is golden brown. Serve hot, with lemon wedges.

bruschetta

Originating from Rome, bruschetta are slices of coarse country bread baked until crisp and slightly charred, then rubbed with garlic and drizzled with olive oil. For centuries, bruschetta has been a staple of the poor, usually eaten to celebrate the new season's olive oil. Nowadays it is typically served as an appetizer, while you wait for your pasta to be ready. Bruschetta is also excellent with fish soups and pan-fried chicken livers. I like to use Pugliese bread.

MAKES 6

6 slices of coarse white Italian bread, about
  1¼ inches thick
2 garlic cloves, peeled and halved

about 6 tablespoons extra virgin olive oil
  for drizzling
sea salt and freshly ground black pepper

1 Preheat a ridged grill pan, and heat the oven to 425°F. Score the bread slices lightly with the point of a small knife in a criss-cross fashion, then grill to toast on both sides.

2 While still hot, rub the toasted surface all over with the cut garlic cloves. Put the toast slices on a baking sheet and bake for 2 minutes to crisp them through.

3 Drizzle about 1 tablespoon extra virgin oil over each slice. Sprinkle generously with pepper and a little salt, then serve.

fava bean purée

A wonderful purée to be enjoyed during the all-too-brief, early-summer fava bean season. You can spread it on crostini moistened with olive oil, or serve the purée piled up in a dish surrounded by crostini. It is also delicious spread on bruschetta (page 21), wonderful in a panino with some pecorino cheese, and it can be served as a dip with crudités. One of my favorite restaurants serves a fava bean purée topped with grilled scallops and roasted cherry tomatoes. When fresh fava beans are unavailable, make the purée with frozen lima beans.

Illustrated on previous page

SERVES 6–8

3¹/₂ cups shelled fresh fava beans or frozen
  baby lima beans
2 garlic cloves, peeled
2 slices crustless white bread
about 2 tablespoons milk
5 tablespoons extra virgin olive oil
sea salt and freshly ground black pepper

FOR THE CROSTINI:
12–16 slices of ciabatta bread
extra virgin olive oil for drizzling

1 Cook the fresh or frozen beans in a saucepan of gently simmering water, to which you have added 1 garlic clove, for about 5 minutes. When the beans are tender, drain them and the garlic, reserving 2 tablespoons of the liquid. Set aside to cool.

2 Place the bread in a bowl and pour on enough milk to moisten it. Slip the fava beans out of their white skins and discard the skins. (This will give you a really creamy purée.)

3 Put the bright emerald-green beans, both garlic cloves, and the bread with its milk into a food processor. Blend to a purée, gradually adding the olive oil through the feed tube. If the purée is very thick, add a little of the reserved bean cooking liquid. Taste and adjust the seasoning.

4 For the crostini, preheat the oven to 350°F. Bake the ciabatta slices until crisp and golden, about 10–12 minutes. Moisten the crostini with a little extra virgin olive oil, then serve topped with the fava bean purée.

chicken liver crostini

In Tuscany, where this dish comes from, the robust chicken liver, garlic, and wine mixture is served on baked ciabatta crostini. If you prefer, you can use bruschetta (page 21) instead, allowing one per person.

SERVES 6–8

9 oz chicken livers
2 tablespoons olive oil
1 celery stalk, minced
1 shallot, peeled and minced
2 small garlic cloves, peeled and chopped
generous handful of flat-leaf parsley, chopped
4 oz (about ½ cup) lean ground beef
1 tablespoon tomato paste

6 tablespoons dry white wine
12–16 slices of ciabatta bread
1 tablespoon capers, rinsed and chopped
2 salted anchovy fillets, rinsed and minced
7 tablespoons unsalted butter
extra virgin olive oil for drizzling
sea salt and freshly ground black pepper

1 Trim the fat and gristle from the chicken livers, then rinse, pat dry with paper towels, and chop finely. Set aside.

2 Heat the olive oil in a saucepan and, when just hot, add the celery, shallot, garlic, and parsley. Cook for about 10 minutes until soft, stirring frequently.

3 Add the chicken livers and ground beef, and cook over a very low heat until the livers have lost their raw color and become crumbly. Mix in the tomato paste and cook for 1 minute.

4 Increase the heat, pour in the wine, and boil to reduce until nearly all of it has evaporated. Lower the heat, and add a little salt and plenty of pepper. Simmer for 30 minutes, adding a little hot water if the mixture becomes too dry.

5 Meanwhile, preheat the oven to 350°F. For the crostini, bake the ciabatta slices until crisp and golden, about 10–12 minutes.

6 Add the capers and anchovies to the chicken liver mixture. Mix in the butter and cook gently for 5 minutes, stirring constantly. Moisten the crostini with a little extra virgin olive oil, then spread with the chicken liver mixture. Serve at once.

simple antipasti

Italians often start their main meal of the day with antipasti—tasty, light morsels that stimulate the palate for the courses to follow. Salamis, prosciutto, and other cold meats are often a feature of antipasti, and seafood dishes are especially popular in coastal areas. Colorful vegetables and salads in sharp dressings bring the tastebuds to anticipatory life, too.

Antipasto has always been one of the most exciting courses for me, as I love the variety of flavors and textures on offer. And I'm delighted to see the increasing range of Italian antipasto foods now available in supermarkets—preserved and dried vegetables, tasty spreads and dips, interesting fresh breads, grissini (breadsticks), cured meats, cheeses, olives, capers, and salted anchovies. With these you can create appetizing antipasti with the minimum of time and effort. Try the following simple ideas.

▲ prosciutto with fresh figs and mozzarella
Drape 2 slices of prosciutto on each serving plate and top with a fresh fig half. Tear some fresh buffalo mozzarella into pieces and place alongside. Dress with a little aged balsamic vinegar and extra virgin olive oil, then sprinkle with a small handful of toasted pine nuts. Season with salt and a generous grind of black pepper, then serve, with grissini and olives.

eggplant and olives on arugula with Parmesan

For each serving, grill or broil 3 thick eggplant slices that have been brushed with olive oil. Arrange on a bed of arugula leaves. Top each eggplant slice with 2 chopped sun-dried tomatoes in oil, a couple of anchovies (rinsed if salted), and some pitted black or green olives. Scatter with some Parmesan cheese shavings, and serve, with a loaf of rustic Italian bread.

roasted pepper and tuna salad

To serve 4–6, roast 2 red and 2 yellow bell peppers at 400°F for 20 minutes; cool. Skin, core, seed, and chop the peppers and 6 plum tomatoes. Tear ½ ciabatta loaf into cubes, put into a bowl, and moisten with 4 tbsp extra virgin olive oil. Add the peppers, tomatoes, and 2 drained, flaked 7-oz cans tuna in water. Add 2 tbsp each chopped parsley, basil, and capers, and 12 pitted black olives. Drizzle with another 4 tbsp oil and 2 tbsp red wine vinegar, season well, toss, and serve.

▲ artichoke, chick pea, and baby spinach salad

To serve 4–6, drain and rinse a 14-oz can of chick peas (garbanzo beans). Drain a 10-oz jar of artichokes in oil and quarter the artichokes. Combine the chick peas and artichokes in a bowl with 1 minced red onion. Add 2 large handfuls of baby spinach leaves and a handful of pitted black olives. For the dressing, whisk the juice of 1 lemon with salt, pepper, and 6 tbsp extra virgin olive oil. Add to the salad and toss to mix. (Tear a little mozzarella over the salad, if desired.)

tomatoes stuffed with crumbs and parsley

Flavorful, ripe tomatoes are essential for this classic Roman antipasto dish, *pomodori ammollicati*. Make it in advance if you like, to allow time for the flavors to combine and intensify. Serve hot, warm, or cool, but not chilled.

SERVES 4

6 large, ripe but firm, tomatoes (preferably with stems)
olive oil for brushing
handful of flat-leaf parsley, chopped
2 garlic cloves, peeled and chopped
1 tablespoon capers, rinsed and chopped
½ small, dried hot chili pepper, crumbled

2 cups fresh white bread crumbs (slightly dry)
1 teaspoon dried oregano
1 tablespoon extra virgin olive oil, plus extra for drizzling
sea salt and freshly ground black pepper
freshly grated Parmesan cheese for serving (optional)

1 Cut the tops off the tomatoes and reserve. Scoop out the core and seeds, then sprinkle the cavities with salt. Lay the tomatoes, cut-side down, on paper towels and let drain for about 30 minutes.

2 Preheat the oven to 375°F. Brush the bottom of a shallow baking dish or roasting pan with a little olive oil. Wipe the inside of the tomatoes with paper towels.

3 Combine the parsley, garlic, capers, chili, bread crumbs, and oregano in a bowl. Mix well, then stir in the extra virgin olive oil. Season with salt and pepper to taste.

4 Arrange the tomatoes, cut-side up, in the prepared dish and spoon in the stuffing. Replace the tomato lids and bake for about 20 minutes until the tomatoes are soft but still whole.

5 If liked, lift the tomato lids, drizzle a little olive oil over the stuffing, and sprinkle lightly with grated Parmesan. Serve hot, warm, or at room temperature.

Sicilian baked eggplants

I love eggplants, and this dish is one of my favorites. The eggplant flesh is scooped out of the skins and mixed with a spicy sausage meat and two favored Sicilian ingredients—pine nuts and currants. This mixture is piled back into the eggplant skins, which are then baked.

SERVES 4

2 medium eggplants

4 tablespoons olive oil, plus extra for drizzling

1 large garlic clove, peeled and crushed

2 shallots, peeled and minced

1 celery stalk, chopped

9 oz spicy fresh pork sausage, skinned

2$^{1}/_{2}$ cups fresh white bread crumbs

2 tablespoons pine nuts

2 tablespoons capers, rinsed and dried

1 egg, beaten

2 teaspoons dried oregano

2 tablespoons freshly grated Parmesan cheese

1 tablespoon currants

1 large ripe tomato, cut into strips

sea salt and freshly ground black pepper

1   Cut the eggplants in half lengthwise. Scoop out the flesh, using a small sharp knife and then a small teaspoon, leaving a thin layer inside the skin. Be careful not to pierce the skin.

2   Chop the eggplant pulp coarsely and place in a colander. Sprinkle with salt, mix well, and set aside to drain for 20 minutes.

3   Heat 3 tablespoons of the olive oil in a frying pan. Add the garlic, shallots, and celery, and sauté over a low heat until soft, stirring frequently. Add the sausage meat, in small pieces, and cook for 20 minutes, turning frequently.

4   Meanwhile, preheat the oven to 350°F. Squeeze the liquid from the eggplant pulp, rinse to remove excess salt, drain, and pat dry with paper towels. Add the eggplant pulp to the pan and fry gently, stirring, for a few minutes. Taste and adjust the seasoning.

5   Add the bread crumbs to the frying pan and cook, stirring, for 2–3 minutes. Stir in the pine nuts and cook for a further 30 seconds, then transfer to a bowl. Add the capers, egg, oregano, Parmesan, currants, and some salt and pepper. Mix thoroughly, then taste and adjust the seasoning.

6   Oil a deep baking dish with the remaining 1 tablespoon olive oil. Pat the inside of the eggplant shells dry, then place side by side in the dish and fill with the sausage mixture. Lay the tomato strips on the top and drizzle with a little olive oil. Pour $^{2}/_{3}$ cup water into the bottom of the dish. Cover with foil and bake for 20 minutes, then remove the foil and bake for 20 minutes longer. Let cool for about 1 hour, then serve the dish warm.

braised shallots

Braised in wine with grapes, these shallots often form part of a spectacular Piedmontese antipasto, served either hot or cold. They may also accompany cold meats, or you can serve them hot with braised meat dishes. In Italy, white, squat onions called *borratine* are used. These are hard to find in this country, so I always use shallots.

SERVES 4

1³/₄ *lb shallots*
3 tablespoons olive oil
2 tablespoons unsalted butter
2 teaspoons tomato paste
1 tablespoon sugar
2 tablespoons red wine vinegar
2 cups seedless black or red grapes
sea salt and freshly ground black pepper

1 Add the shallots to a pan of boiling water, bring back to a boil, and blanch for 1 minute. Drain, then remove the skins and root ends, taking care to keep the root base intact, as this holds the shallot together during cooking.

2 Heat the olive oil and butter in a large sauté pan. Add the shallots and sauté for about 12 minutes until golden, shaking the pan frequently.

3 Dissolve the tomato paste in 2 teaspoons of hot water and add to the pan along with the sugar, vinegar, grapes, and some salt and pepper. Cook, uncovered, for about 25 minutes until the shallots are tender and a nice brown color, adding a little water if necessary. Serve the shallots hot or cold, but not chilled.

stuffed mushrooms

A wonderful combination of intense flavors—dried porcini, anchovy, nutmeg, garlic, and marjoram—is piled into big portobello mushrooms and baked to serve as an antipasto. It's a very light and tasty first course, which can also be served as a side dish with meat main dishes.

SERVES 4

2 oz dried porcini mushrooms

4 portobello mushrooms

2 anchovy fillets in oil, drained

1 garlic clove, peeled

handful of marjoram leaves

2 cups fresh white bread crumbs

pinch of freshly grated nutmeg

2 tablespoons olive oil, plus extra for drizzling

handful of flat-leaf parsley, minced

sea salt and freshly ground black pepper

1 Soak the dried porcini in warm water to cover for 10 minutes. Drain and pat dry with paper towels. (Save the soaking water to use as stock for another dish, if you like.)

2 Preheat the oven to 400°F. Gently wipe the portobello mushrooms with damp paper towels to clean them. Detach the stems and reserve.

3 Chop the soaked porcini, mushroom stems, anchovies, garlic, and marjoram together. Tip into a bowl and add the bread crumbs, nutmeg, and salt and pepper to taste. Mix thoroughly.

4 Heat the olive oil in a frying pan over a medium heat. Add the mushroom and bread crumb mixture, and sauté for 5 minutes.

5 Lay the portobello mushroom caps on an oiled baking sheet, hollow-side up. Season lightly with salt, then fill them with the crumb mixture. Sprinkle parsley on top of each stuffed mushroom and drizzle with a little olive oil. Bake for 10–15 minutes until soft. Serve at room temperature.

duck breasts with balsamic vinegar

Duck is very popular in Italy, particularly around the Puccini lake near Lucca, where the locals shoot a lot of wild duck. There is a resurgence in the popularity of farmed duck too, because of its fine flavor. It's particularly delicious dressed with balsamic vinegar and served with my favorite broiled radicchio, or on a bed of crisp arugula leaves.

SERVES 6

2 boneless duck breast halves, each about 14 oz

3 heads of radicchio

3 tablespoons aged balsamic vinegar, or a little more to taste

sea salt and freshly ground black pepper

1 Cut the duck breasts across in half. Score the skin with the tip of a small sharp knife, then rub with salt and pepper.

2 Heat a heavy-based frying pan. Place the duck breasts in the pan, skin-side down, and cook over a medium heat for about 9 minutes, depending on thickness. Pour most of the rendered fat from the pan. (Save it for sautéeing potatoes, if you like.)

3 Meanwhile, preheat the broiler. Quarter the radicchio and place on a lightly oiled baking sheet. Broil for 7–10 minutes, turning occasionally, until slightly charred all over.

4 Spoon 1 tablespoon balsamic vinegar over the duck breasts, then turn them over and cook for 2 minutes on the other side. Lift out the duck breasts onto a board, cover with foil, and set aside in a warm place to rest for 10 minutes.

5 In the meantime, add the remaining balsamic vinegar and 3 tablespoons warm water to the frying pan and stir well to deglaze, scraping up the sediment from the bottom of the pan. Taste for seasoning and add a little more balsamic vinegar if required.

6 Carve the duck across into ½-inch slices and arrange on warm plates, with the broiled radicchio alongside. Drizzle the balsamic pan juices over the duck breast slices and serve.

mozzarella fritters with roasted cherry tomatoes

For these intensely flavored cheesy bites, grated mozzarella and Parmesan are tossed with flour, bound with beaten egg, then fried and served with roasted cherry tomatoes on the vine. The mozzarella must be removed from its pack, drained, and refrigerated for 24 hours before shredding, so that it can dry out a little. The fritters are highly popular with children.

SERVES 4

9 oz mozzarella cheese, drained and dried
  slightly (see above)
1¼ cups freshly grated Parmesan cheese
2 tablespoons Italian "00" flour
1 egg, lightly beaten
generous handful of basil leaves, torn
1 garlic clove, peeled and crushed
4 tablespoons olive oil
sea salt and freshly ground black pepper
FOR THE ROASTED CHERRY TOMATOES:
9 oz cherry tomatoes, on the vine
olive oil for drizzling

1 Preheat the oven to 350°F. Coarsely shred the mozzarella and place in a bowl. Add the Parmesan and flour, and toss to mix, then add the beaten egg to bind, mixing thoroughly.

2 Add the torn basil, garlic, and some salt and pepper, and mix well. With damp hands, shape the mixture into balls the size of a walnut. Place on a tray and chill for 30 minutes.

3 Place the cherry tomatoes (still on the vine) on an oiled baking sheet, drizzle with a little olive oil, and roast for 20 minutes until the skins split.

4 Meanwhile, heat the 4 tablespoons olive oil in a large frying pan. Fry the mozzarella fritters, in batches, for about 10 minutes, turning, until golden all over. Remove with a slotted spoon and drain on paper towels. Keep warm until they are all cooked.

5 Drizzle the roasted cherry tomatoes with a little more olive oil and season well. Serve the fritters hot, with the roasted tomatoes.

Piedmontese fondue

Fontina, the best known cheese from the Valle d'Aosta in northern Italy, was originally made at Monte Fontina, hence the name. It is the main ingredient of a classic *fonduta piemontese*. The other characteristic ingredient is the white truffle of Alba. Fresh white truffle is prohibitively expensive, but you can buy truffle paste made with white truffles and porcini, which works very well in a *fonduta*. Crostini are served for dipping into the *fonduta*. Alternatively, you can use cubes of slightly dry, coarse-textured bread, or thick slices of polenta (page 96).

SERVES 4

14 oz Italian fontina cheese
9 fl oz (1 cup + 2 tablespoons) whole milk
1/2 cup (1 stick) unsalted butter
4 egg yolks
freshly ground black pepper
1 tablespoon truffle paste (optional)
FOR THE CROSTINI:
12–16 slices of ciabatta bread

1 About 4 hours ahead of serving, cut the fontina into small dice. Place in a bowl, add enough of the milk to cover the cheese, and set aside.

2 Preheat the oven to 350°F. Put the butter into a large, heatproof bowl set over a pan of simmering water, and add the fontina and all of the milk. Cook, stirring constantly, until the cheese has melted, about 10 minutes.

3 Meanwhile, for the crostini, bake the ciabatta slices until crisp and golden, about 10–12 minutes.

4 Beat the egg yolks into the smooth cheese mixture, one at a time. Continue to cook over the pan of simmering water, beating constantly, until the *fonduta* is the consistency of thick cream. Season with a generous grind of black pepper and remove from the heat. If you happen to be adding truffle paste, stir it in at this point.

5 Transfer the *fonduta* to warm individual bowls and serve the crostini to accompany.

2 soups

minestrone

This "soup of the kitchen," or *minestrone della cucina*, is one born out of necessity, and the ingredients are determined by the contents of the *dispensa* (pantry). This one includes carrots, peas, celery, onion, vermouth, spaghetti broken into small pieces, and plenty of fresh parsley, but you can use whatever vegetables are around in the kitchen. A few strands of spaghetti are vital. Serve with bruschetta (page 21).

SERVES 6

6 cups chicken broth (page 47)
2 tablespoons olive oil
1 onion, peeled and minced
3 bay leaves
2 garlic cloves, peeled and chopped
handful of flat-leaf parsley, chopped
2 celery stalks, sliced
2 large carrots, peeled and roughly chopped
1 parsnip, peeled and roughly chopped
2 leeks, washed, trimmed, and finely sliced
1¹/₂ cups fresh or frozen green peas
  (preferably fresh)
12 strands of spaghetti, broken into
  short lengths
2 tablespoons sweet vermouth
sea salt and freshly ground black pepper

1 Pour the chicken broth into a large saucepan and bring to a simmer.

2 Heat the olive oil in another large saucepan, add the onion, and sauté gently for about 5 minutes until golden. Add the bay leaves, garlic, and parsley, and stir. Add the celery, carrots, parsnip, and leeks, and sauté until slightly softened.

3 Add the warmed chicken broth to the pan and bring to a boil. Add the peas, pasta, and vermouth, and simmer for 20 minutes until the vegetables are all tender. Taste for seasoning, then serve, in warm bowls with rustic bread.

lettuce in broth

Stuffed vegetables are a source of pride in the cooking of Liguria. Here lettuce leaves are stuffed with dried porcini, Parmesan, fresh marjoram, and bread crumbs, then cooked in a fine broth.

SERVES 6

1 oz dried porcini mushrooms

3 cups coarse, fresh white bread crumbs
  (slightly dry)

3 tablespoons milk

6 small romaine hearts

2 garlic cloves, peeled and chopped

2 tablespoons chopped marjoram leaves

2 eggs, beaten

¼ cup freshly grated Parmesan cheese

1 egg white, beaten

6 or 12 slices of firm, coarse-textured bread

6 tablespoons extra virgin olive oil

6 cups chicken or vegetable broth
  (page 47)

sea salt and freshly ground black pepper

1 Preheat the oven to 350°F. Soak the dried porcini in warm water for 10 minutes, then drain and chop. Soak the bread crumbs in the milk for 5 minutes, then squeeze dry. Discard any discolored outer leaves from the romaine hearts.

2 Chop two of the romaine hearts and place in a bowl. Add the porcini, garlic, bread crumbs, and marjoram. Mix in the eggs, Parmesan, and seasoning.

3 Blanch the remaining romaine hearts in a pan of boiling water for a few seconds. Drain, then open carefully and fill with the prepared stuffing. Close, brushing with the beaten egg white to seal.

4 Brush the bread slices liberally with 5 tablespoons olive oil, place on a baking sheet, and toast in the oven for about 10 minutes. Meanwhile, heat the remaining olive oil and 4 tablespoons of the broth in a wide saucepan, add the stuffed romaine hearts, and cook, covered, for a few minutes over a low heat, turning occasionally. Bring the rest of the broth to a boil in another pan. Put one or two toast slices into each warm soup bowl, add a romaine heart, and ladle the hot broth over.

Tuscan leek and tomato soup

This is a variant on the classic Tuscan *pappa con pomodoro*, a simple soup, made here with fresh tomatoes, leeks, the best possible broth, and the finest extra virgin olive oil. The inclusion of bread is typically Italian—even when stale, bread is never wasted and it adds texture to a soup.

SERVES 6

8 young leeks, trimmed

4 tablespoons olive oil

1¹/₂ lb ripe tomatoes

¹/₂ teaspoon dried chili flakes

9 oz crusty day-old bread

3 cups chicken or vegetable broth
  (page 47)

6 basil leaves

extra virgin olive oil for drizzling

sea salt and freshly ground black pepper

1 Wash the leeks well under cold running water. Drain, then mince. Heat the olive oil in a large saucepan, add the leeks, and fry gently for 10 minutes.

2 Meanwhile, blend the tomatoes in a blender or food processor to a purée (then press through a strainer to remove skins and seeds, if you prefer, though this isn't essential). Add to the leeks along with the chili flakes and some salt and pepper. Bring to a boil and simmer for 20 minutes.

3 Break the bread into small pieces and add to the pan. Stir well and simmer gently for 5 minutes. Pour in the broth, mix well, and simmer for 10 minutes longer.

4 Pour the soup into warm bowls and add a basil leaf to each serving. Drizzle with a little extra virgin olive oil and serve.

la ribollita

A thick Tuscan soup made with good day-old bread, assorted vegetables, and beans. It is traditionally made one day ahead, hence the name *ribollita*, which means "re-boiled." The vegetables here are only a suggestion: you can use any combination as long as you have the basic *soffritto* flavoring of onion, celery, and carrot. For instance, you could substitute Savoy cabbage for the cavolo nero, and use a 14-oz can of cannellini beans instead of dried beans.

SERVES 6

1 cup dried cannellini beans, soaked in
  cold water overnight
4 tablespoons olive oil
1 large onion, peeled and finely sliced
4 carrots, peeled and chopped
4 celery stalks, chopped
4 leeks, washed, trimmed, and chopped
2 garlic cloves, peeled and crushed
9 oz cavolo nero, tough stems discarded,
  leaves chopped
8 ripe tomatoes, peeled, seeded, and
  quartered

1 dried hot chili pepper, crumbled (with seeds)
6 cups vegetable broth (page 47) or water
small handful of chopped flat-leaf parsley
1 rosemary sprig, minced
2 bay leaves
sea salt and freshly ground black pepper

FOR SERVING:
8 slices of country-style bread
extra virgin olive oil (preferably new season's,
  estate bottled) for drizzling
3 tablespoons chopped flat-leaf parsley

1 Drain the cannellini beans and rinse under fresh cold water. Place in a large saucepan, cover generously with cold water, and bring to a boil. Lower the heat, cover, and simmer gently for about 1½ hours until the beans are just tender.

2 Heat half the olive oil in a large, heavy-based pan, add the onion, cover, and sweat for 5 minutes to soften. Add the carrots, celery, leeks, and half of the garlic, and sweat for a further 5 minutes. Add the cabbage, tomatoes, and chili, and stir to coat in the oil. Add the beans and vegetable broth or water, and simmer for 30 minutes or until the beans are soft.

3 Ladle one-third of the soup mixture into a blender or food processor and blend to a purée. Pour this back into the pan and stir to mix.

4 Heat the remaining 2 tablespoons olive oil in a separate pan and sauté the other crushed garlic clove with the chopped herbs and bay leaves until lightly browned. Add to the soup. Let cool, then refrigerate for 24 hours.

5 The next day, warm the soup through in an uncovered pan and check the seasoning. Place a slice of bread in each warm soup bowl and ladle the ribollita over the top. Drizzle with a generous amount of extra virgin olive oil and sprinkle with sea salt and chopped parsley to serve.

Italian broths

A good, fine-flavored *brodo*—broth or stock—is paramount in Italian cooking. It is the basis for most soups and savory sauces, and is absolutely vital in the making of risottos. The ingredients, however, have to be of the finest quality.

A chicken broth really should be made with a whole chicken, although a slightly less flavorsome broth can be made with a raw carcass (or you could use a cooked carcass if you have one left over). A fish broth must be made with white fish bones; oily fish are not suitable. When you buy cleaned fish from the fishmonger or fresh fish counter, ask for the bones (and perhaps an extra white fish head or two for additional flavor).

With any of the following broths, the aromatic vegetables, herbs, and spices can be varied to taste, but ideally you should use a classic flavoring base—or *soffritto*—of onion, celery, carrot, and parsley.

▲ **fish broth**

To make 6 cups, put 2¼ lb white fish heads and bones into a large pan. Add 2 peeled onions (each one stuck with 5 cloves), 2 carrots, 2 celery stalks, 2 bay leaves, 10 black peppercorns, 1½ tsp salt, and 2 cups dry white wine. Add 8 cups water and bring to a boil. Boil, uncovered, for 30 minutes until well reduced. Strain the liquid, discarding the bones and aromatics. Cool, then chill. Use within 1–2 days or freeze.

chicken broth

To make about 6 cups, rinse a 3-lb chicken in cold water and cut off any visible fat. Bring 3½ quarts water to a boil in a very large saucepan or stockpot over a high heat. Add the chicken to the pan along with 2 peeled onions, 2 celery stalks, and 1 large potato, peeled and quartered. Add 3 bay leaves and a handful of parsley (leaves and stems). Bring to a boil and boil rapidly for 5 minutes. Reduce the heat to low and

▼ vegetable broth

To make about 6 cups, heat 1 tbsp olive oil with 3 tbsp unsalted butter in a large saucepan or stockpot. Add 3 crushed garlic cloves and fry gently for 2 minutes. Coarsely chop 1 large onion, 4 leeks, 2 carrots, and 2 celery stalks. Add to the pan with 1 halved fennel bulb, a handful of chopped flat-leaf parsley, 4 bay leaves, and 2 thyme sprigs. Cook over a low heat, stirring constantly, until softened, but not

simmer very slowly, uncovered, for about 2 hours. Skim off any scum from the surface from time to time. Remove the chicken, then strain the broth. Let cool, then chill. Once chilled, remove the solidified fat that has accumulated on the surface. Keep refrigerated and use within 4–5 days, or freeze.

browned. Add 3 quarts water and bring to a boil. Reduce the heat, cover, and simmer for 1 hour. Strain the stock and return to the pan. Boil rapidly until reduced by half. Let cool. Keep refrigerated and use within 3 days, or freeze.

fennel soup with roasted tomatoes

In the high bleak mountains of Sardinia, the wild greens and herbs that grow in abundance everywhere are used in cooking, both by the itinerant shepherds and in Sardinian homes. Small wild fennel bulbs are traditional here, but cultivated fennel works perfectly well.
Illustrated on previous page

SERVES 4

4 fennel bulbs

1 tablespoon olive oil

6 cups vegetable broth (page 47)

1 teaspoon fennel seeds

handful of flat-leaf parsley, minced

sea salt and freshly ground black pepper

FOR SERVING:

7 oz roasted cherry tomatoes (page 36)

1 Trim the fennel bulbs; reserve the feathery fronds but discard the stems and tough outer layers. Slice the bulbs thinly, then mince. Chop the feathery tops as well; set aside.

2 Heat the olive oil in a large pan, add the minced fennel, and cook over a low heat for 10 minutes. Add the broth, fennel seeds, and seasoning. Bring to a boil and simmer for 30 minutes.

3 Stir in the chopped parsley and ladle the soup into warm bowls. Top with the roasted cherry tomatoes and fennel fronds to serve.

onion and chick pea soup

This tasty soup of onions, chick peas, tomatoes, bacon, and bread originates from the Marches. It keeps well and tastes even better a day or two after it is made.

SERVES 6

1 cup dried chick peas, soaked overnight

12 oz ripe tomatoes

4 tablespoons olive oil

2¼ lb onions, peeled and sliced

1 celery stalk, chopped

⅓ cup diced bacon

handful of basil leaves, torn

6 slices of firm, coarse-textured bread

sea salt and freshly ground black pepper

1 Drain and rinse the chick peas. Purée the tomatoes in a food mill, or use a blender and then strain.

2 Heat the olive oil in a large saucepan, add the onions, celery, and bacon, and fry gently for about 5 minutes until the onion is translucent. Add the puréed tomatoes, chick peas, and 4 cups water. Bring to a boil, lower the heat, and simmer for 2 hours. Season and add add most of the basil.

3 When ready to serve, toast the bread slices and place a slice in each warm soup bowl. Pour the hot soup on top and sprinkle with the remaining torn basil.

farro and bean soup

Farro, a form of spelt or soft wheat, is an ancient grain that was grown and eaten by the Romans. It is now mainly cultivated in the Garfagnana region of Tuscany, where this protein-rich soup originated. Farro has a great texture that readily absorbs flavors, such as the *soffritto* (flavoring base) of carrot, celery, and onion. Combined with borlotti beans, it makes for a wonderfully satisfying soup.

SERVES 6

1½ cups dried borlotti beans, soaked in cold
  water overnight
7 oz farro, soaked in cold water overnight
2 white onions, peeled
6 sage leaves
3 garlic cloves, peeled
4 tablespoons olive oil

1 red onion, peeled and minced
2 carrots, scraped and diced
2–4 celery stalks, diced
handful of flat-leaf parsley, chopped
1¼ cups canned Italian plum tomatoes, with
  their juice
sea salt and freshly ground black pepper
extra virgin olive oil for drizzling

1   Drain and rinse the borlotti beans, then place in a large saucepan with 1 whole white onion, 3 sage leaves, 1 garlic clove, and enough water to cover by at least 2 inches. Bring to a boil, lower the heat, cover, and simmer for 1 hour or until tender.

2   When the beans are cooked, pass half of the contents of the pan through a food mill, or purée in a blender or food processor, and set aside. Keep the whole beans in the pan.

3   Mince the other white onion and the remaining garlic. Heat the olive oil in a large saucepan and add the minced red and white onions, the carrots, celery, and garlic. Stir well, then add most of the parsley, the remaining 3 sage leaves, the tomatoes, and 3 tablespoons water. Continue to cook, stirring occasionally, for 10 minutes.

4   Drain and rinse the farro, and add to the tomato mixture along with the whole borlotti beans. Bring to a simmer and simmer over a low heat for 20 minutes. Add the puréed bean mixture and season with salt and pepper. Heat, stirring, until warmed through.

5   Taste and adjust the seasoning, then ladle into warm bowls. Serve topped with a generous drizzle of extra virgin olive oil and the remaining chopped parsley.

Livorno fish soup

Livorno is a city by the sea in Tuscany, famous for its beautiful 17th-century port. It is also renowned for its robust fish soup or stew, which is made from a variety of Mediterranean fish.

SERVES 6

4 tablespoons olive oil

1 onion, peeled and minced

1 carrot, peeled and minced

1 celery stalk, minced

handful of flat-leaf parsley, chopped

small piece of hot red chili pepper, minced

1 lb raw shrimp in shell

2 medium squid, cleaned and sliced into rings

1 cup dry white wine

12 oz plum tomatoes, peeled and chopped

1 lb fresh mussels, cleaned

1 lb fresh hardshell clams, cleaned

1½ lb porgy or scup, filleted and skinned

1 small cooked lobster, cleaned (optional)

salt and freshly ground black pepper

FOR SERVING:

6 thin slices of firm, coarse-textured bread

2 garlic cloves, peeled and crushed

1   Heat the olive oil in a large pan, add the onion, carrot, celery, parsley, and chili, and cook over a medium heat until the onion begins to color. Stir in the shrimp and squid, and cook gently for 10 minutes, then remove the shrimp and set aside. Add the wine, ½ cup hot water, and the tomatoes, and simmer for 10 minutes longer. Season with salt. Remove the squid and set aside.

2   Put the mussels and clams into a steamer over boiling water, cover tightly, and steam just until open, about 3–5 minutes. Discard any that remain closed.

3   Meanwhile, strain the vegetables and cooking liquid through a fine sieve into a saucepan, rubbing with the back of a ladle. Add the porgy fillets and simmer until opaque, about 4–5 minutes. Add all the seafood to the pan, including the lobster if using. Heat through gently and check the seasoning. In the meantime, toast the bread slices and spread with the garlic. Place in warm soup bowls, ladle the fish soup over the garlic toasts, and serve.

chicken soup with poached egg and Parmesan

Known as *zuppa alla pavese*, this dish comes from Padua—Romeo and Juliet country. It is a great soup for a cold winter's evening, being substantial, interesting, and very tasty. A good homemade broth is essential.

SERVES 6

6 cups chicken broth (page 47)
1 bay leaf
6 thin slices of day-old, coarse-textured bread
6 eggs
sea salt and freshly ground black pepper
FOR SERVING:
handful of flat-leaf parsley, minced
1/2 cup freshly grated Parmesan cheese
freshly grated nutmeg, to taste

1 Heat the chicken broth in a large, wide pan. Add the bay leaf and simmer gently over a medium heat for 10 minutes, then discard the bay leaf and check the seasoning. In the meantime, toast the bread slices.

2 One at a time, break the eggs into a cup and gently pour into the hot broth. The egg whites will immediately coagulate. Continue to poach until the whites are set.

3 Put a slice of toasted bread into each warm soup bowl. Using a slotted spoon, carefully place a poached egg on top, then ladle in the fragrant broth. Scatter the parsley and Parmesan on top and sprinkle with a little grated nutmeg. Serve at once.

lentil soup with pancetta and potatoes

This flavorsome soup of lentils, pancetta, potatoes, parsley, and tomatoes is wonderfully enticing. I would always use Castelluccio lentils, which are hand-grown and -picked in Italy. However, as an alternative, you can use the French lentilles de Puy, which lend a slightly different texture and flavor.

SERVES 6

10 new potatoes, scrubbed

3 bay leaves

1 cup diced pancetta

2 garlic cloves, peeled and crushed

1¼ cups small green lentils

3 tablespoons olive oil

3 cups bottled tomato passata (purée), or 28 oz
  canned crushed tomatoes

sea salt and freshly ground black pepper

FOR SERVING:

½ cup freshly grated Parmesan cheese

generous handful of flat-leaf parsley, chopped

extra virgin olive oil for drizzling

1 Cut the potatoes into even-sized cubes and put into a medium saucepan. Pour in 4 cups boiling water and add the bay leaves and some salt and pepper. Bring to a simmer and cook for 10 minutes.

2 In the meantime, fry the pancetta dice in a frying pan over a medium heat, turning frequently, until golden.

3 Add the pancetta to the potatoes, along with the garlic, lentils, olive oil, passata or crushed tomatoes, and some pepper. Return to a simmer, cover, and cook for 40 minutes. Adjust the seasoning.

4 Serve sprinkled with Parmesan and parsley, and topped with a generous drizzle of good, fruity extra virgin olive oil.

potato and sausage soup

This comforting, hearty soup comes from Emilia-Romagna, the gastronomic center of Italy. It is made from a purée of potatoes and onions, with the addition of sausage. The semolina shouldn't be omitted as it adds a good texture, but you can vary the flavor by using different types of sausages. Freshly grated Parmesan and plenty of parsley are essential.

SERVES 6

6 cups chicken broth (page 47)
3 medium potatoes, peeled and sliced
1 onion, peeled and minced
$\frac{1}{2}$ cup milk
1 tablespoon semolina
2 cooked Italian sausages, thinly sliced
sea salt and freshly ground black pepper

FOR SERVING:

handful of flat-leaf parsley, minced
freshly grated Parmesan cheese, to taste

1 Heat the chicken broth in a large saucepan, then add the sliced potatoes and onion. Cook over a medium heat for 10–15 minutes or until the potato is soft.

2 Using a slotted spoon, remove the potato and onion from the stock and pass through a food mill, or mash until smooth, then return to the liquid.

3 Add the milk and sprinkle the semolina over the soup, stirring constantly. Cook over a medium heat, stirring, for 10 minutes. Add the sausage slices and cook for a further 10 minutes. Season with salt and pepper to taste.

4 Ladle the soup into warm bowls and scatter on the parsley. Sprinkle with Parmesan and serve.

3 breads and pizzas

ciabatta

Olive-oil-enriched, crisp, and flavorful, this is the bread that all bakers aspire to make, yet it really is quite simple. The starting point is a "biga," a fermented yeast starter, which makes the dough sweeter and smoother, and gives the loaf its characteristic open texture.

MAKES 4 LOAVES

1 cake (0.6-oz) compressed fresh yeast, or
  1 teaspoon quick-rising active dry yeast
4 cups all-purpose or white bread flour
1 tablespoon fine sea salt
¹/₂ recipe of biga (see right)
olive oil for oiling

1 Measure 1¼ cups warm water. In a small bowl, blend the fresh yeast (or simply mix the dry yeast) with 3 tablespoons of this water.

2 Combine the flour and salt in a large bowl, make a well in the center, and add the biga, yeast liquid, and remaining water. Mix together to form a sticky dough, then knead well to develop the elasticity. As it is wet, the dough will adhere to your hand in large elastic lumps, but persevere; or use a mixer to knead it if you prefer. Do the stretch test (see below) to check the dough is ready.

3 Liberally oil a large bowl, drop in the dough, and turn it carefully to bathe in olive oil. Leave in a warm place until doubled or even trebled in volume, 1½–2 hours or possibly even longer.

4 Oil two baking sheets. Gently ease the puffy dough onto a well-floured surface, avoiding knocking out the air. With floured hands and a dough scraper or sharp knife, cut into 4 pieces. As you pick each piece up, gently roll in the flour and give it a hearty stretch to elongate it to the classic slipper shape, then place on the baking sheets. Cover and let rise for an hour.

5 Toward the end of this time, preheat the oven to 400°F. After rising, the loaves will still look flat, but they will spring up in the oven. Bake them for 20 minutes until golden. Cool on a wire rack and eat warm.

stretch test   To check whether a dough has been kneaded enough for the gluten to develop elasticity, stretch a piece of dough between your fingers. It should behave like an elastic band, not ripping or breaking. This is what I call "the stretch test," vital when making breads.

biga

This fermented yeast starter is the cornerstone of Italian breads. It enhances the performance of the yeast in the dough, helps to develop that wonderful yeasty aroma, and gives a characteristic open texture. Use fresh yeast if possible. You won't use all of the biga for the ciabatta or any of my other breads, but you can keep the rest in the refrigerator to make another loaf—for up to 3 days (no longer, or it will become acidic).

MAKES ABOUT 2¼ LB

1 cake (0.6-oz) compressed fresh yeast, or
  1 teaspoon quick-rising active dry yeast
5 cups all-purpose or white bread flour

1 Measure 1¾ cups warm water. In a small bowl, blend the fresh yeast (or simply mix dry yeast) with a little of this water.

2 Mix all the biga ingredients together in a large bowl and beat with a spoon or your hands until you have a smooth, loose dough. You should feel the elasticity as the gluten develops. Cover and let stand at room temperature for 12–24 hours.

olive and rosemary focaccia

This Italian classic bread is flavored with caramelized onion and garlic, and topped with olives, sea salt, and rosemary before baking. It is best served warm, drizzled with new season's olive oil.

MAKES 1 LARGE LOAF

2 large rosemary sprigs

2 tablespoons olive oil

1 onion, peeled, halved, and sliced

2 garlic cloves, peeled and minced

10 black olives, pitted and halved
   lengthwise

coarse sea salt and coarsely ground black pepper

FOR THE DOUGH:

1 cake (0.6-oz) compressed fresh yeast, or
   1 teaspoon quick-rising active dry yeast

2½ cups all-purpose or white bread flour

1 teaspoon fine sea salt

¼ cup whole-wheat flour

4 oz (¹⁄₉ of recipe) biga (page 61)

olive oil for oiling

1   Mince one-third of the rosemary leaves; keep another third of them whole; divide the rest into tiny sprigs and set aside for the topping. Heat the olive oil in a frying pan and sauté the onion and minced rosemary for 10 minutes. Add the garlic and cook over a medium heat until the mixture caramelizes. Tip into a bowl and let cool.

2   For the dough, dissolve the yeast in 7½ fl oz warm water. Mix the white flour with the salt on the work surface, pile into a mound, and make a well in the center. Add the whole-wheat flour, biga, and yeast liquid to the well, then gradually draw in the white flour with your hands and mix to a dough, adding a little extra water if necessary.

3   Knead the dough for 10 minutes until smooth and elastic, then add half the caramelized onion and continue to knead for 10 minutes. Do the stretch test to check that the dough is ready (see page 60). Place in a lightly oiled large bowl and turn the dough to coat. Cover with a dish towel and leave in a warm place for 2 hours or until almost doubled in bulk.

4   Tip the dough onto a lightly floured surface and gently knead into a round ball. Place on a well-oiled large baking sheet. Cover and let rest for 15 minutes, then flatten the dough with the palm of your hand to an 8-inch round.

5   Mix the rosemary leaves with the remaining onion mixture and spread evenly over the surface of the dough. Season generously with pepper. Cover to prevent a skin from forming and let rise for 2 hours.

6   Preheat the oven to 400°F. Stud the dough with the olives and scatter coarse sea salt evenly over the top. Bake for 15–18 minutes until golden. Transfer to a wire rack to cool slightly and serve warm, scattered with rosemary sprigs.

semolina bread rolls

These rolls come from Puglia in southern Italy. Semolina gives a rich color and a slightly grainy texture and crust. Flavor the dough with a handful of chopped fresh herbs (or a sprinkling of dried), if desired. Perfect for breakfast, these rolls also make delicious *panini* (pages 68–9).

MAKES 12 ROLLS
1 cake (0.6-oz) compressed fresh yeast, or
  1 teaspoon quick-rising active dry yeast
2¼ cups all-purpose or white bread flour
1²/₃ cups semolina

2 teaspoons coarsely ground black pepper
4 oz (¹/₉ of recipe) biga (page 61)
1 tablespoon fine sea salt
olive oil for oiling
2 tablespoons coarse sea salt for sprinkling

1 Dissolve the yeast in 13 fl oz warm water. Combine the flour, semolina, and black pepper on a work surface and pile into a mound. Make a well in the center and add the yeast water and biga. Mix with your hand until all the ingredients are well combined—this will take about 5 minutes.

2 Add the fine salt and knead the dough for 10 minutes until smooth and elastic. Do the stretch test to check that the dough is ready (see page 60). Place the dough in a lightly oiled large bowl, cover with plastic wrap, and leave in a warm place until doubled in size, about 2 hours.

3 Punch down the dough in the bowl, cover again, and let rise for 45 minutes. This second rising will give the dough more strength.

4 Tip the dough onto a lightly floured surface and cut into 12 pieces, using a dough scraper or sharp knife. Shape into balls, place on a lightly oiled baking sheet, and let rise for another hour.

5 Preheat the oven to 400°F. Using a sharp knife, cut a cross on the top of each roll, then sprinkle liberally with coarse salt. Bake for 20 minutes, opening the oven door slightly for the last 5 minutes— this makes the rolls crisper. Cool on a wire rack and eat warm.

honey bread

Sweetened with honey and dried fruit, and enriched with eggs, this bread will keep well for a day or two. The combination of honey and anise seed is a good one, but you can leave out the anise seed if you're not keen on the taste. Delicious at teatime, this sweet bread toasts well too.

MAKES 1 LARGE LOAF

2 cakes (0.6-oz each) compressed fresh yeast, or
  2 teaspoons quick-rising active dry yeast
9 fl oz (1 cup + 2 tablespoons) warm whole milk
3/4 cup thin honey
2 tablespoons melted unsalted butter, cooled
2 tablespoons olive oil, plus extra for oiling
1 egg, beaten
1/2 tablespoon fine sea salt

2 tablespoons anise seed
1 tablespoon finely grated lemon zest
4 cups all-purpose or white bread flour, plus
  extra if needed

FOR THE FILLING AND TOPPING:

1/3 cup raisins
1/3 cup finely chopped walnuts
1/4 cup finely chopped prunes
3 tablespoons thin honey

1 Dissolve the yeast in 1/2 cup warm water in a large bowl, then leave for 10 minutes.

2 Add the milk, honey, melted butter, olive oil, egg, salt, anise seed, and lemon zest to the yeast liquid and stir well.

3 Add the flour and mix with your hands to obtain a ball of dough. If the dough is sticky, mix in a little extra flour. Knead well for 10 minutes to form a soft, smooth, elastic dough. Do the stretch test (see page 60) to check that it is ready. Cover and let rise for 1 1/2 hours or until doubled in size.

4 In a small bowl, mix together the raisins, walnuts, and prunes. Punch down the dough and turn it onto a floured surface. Knead for 2–3 minutes, then roll out to a 16-inch round. Using a brush, spread 2 tablespoons of the honey over the dough and sprinkle with three-fourths of the fruit and nut mixture.

5 Roll the dough up to enclose the filling and form a 16-inch-long loaf about 3 inches thick. Press the ends together to seal, or the honey will seep out. Lift onto a lightly oiled baking sheet, cover, and let rise for 40–60 minutes.

6 Toward the end of this time, preheat the oven to 400°F. Bake the loaf for 30 minutes until the crust is golden brown. Transfer to a wire rack and brush with the remaining honey, then sprinkle the rest of the nut and fruit mixture on top. Cool before serving.

panini

Bread is the "staff of life" in Italy, and to describe someone as *buono come il pane*—as good, kind, warm-hearted, and generous as bread—is a great compliment! It plays a part in virtually every Italian meal, but also figures throughout the day: a panino might be eaten instead of breakfast, for example, or as a mid-morning or afternoon snack.

Panino literally means a bread roll, but nowadays it usually refers to a filled roll, a *panino imbottito*, and anything less like a sandwich would be hard to imagine. An Italian *panino* is a truly wonderful marriage of tasty filling ingredients and irresistible crisp, crusty bread. It is either eaten cold or hot—after warming in a salamander or in a low oven.

Ciabatta loaves and rolls, available from many supermarkets, are convenient bases for *panini*, but you could also use sfilatino or focaccia, or homemade breads such as the semolina rolls on page 64.

▲ mozzarella and baby spinach ciabatta

To serve 2, cut a half ciabatta loaf in two, then split each horizontally. Moisten the insides with extra virgin olive oil. Lay 3 baby spinach leaves on each ciabatta base and add 6 pitted black olives and 2 thin slices of red onion. Cover with 2 generous slices of buffalo mozzarella and 3 drained anchovy fillets in oil. Top with another 3 spinach leaves and season with salt and pepper. Cover with the tops and press down lightly. Heat to serve, if desired.

Taleggio, artichoke, and arugula ciabatta

To serve 4–5, split a whole ciabatta loaf in half horizontally and drizzle the cut surfaces with extra virgin olive oil. Layer 9 oz thinly sliced Taleggio cheese on the base and top with a handful of arugula leaves. Cover with 1 cup drained, sliced artichoke hearts (bottled in oil). Season well. Position the top of the loaf and press down lightly. Heat through, if desired. Cut into sections to serve.

cherry tomato, red onion, and speck panini

To serve 1, divide a ciabatta roll in half and moisten the insides with extra virgin olive oil. Place 4 halved cherry tomatoes on the base and top with ¼ red onion, thinly sliced. Cover with 2 slices speck (smoked, salt-cured, air-dried ham). Finish with 3 slices of smoked scamorza cheese (or mozzarella). Season generously with pepper, but lightly with salt. Position the top of the roll, press down lightly, and heat, if desired.

▲ prosciutto, roasted pepper, and radicchio panini

To serve 1, split a ciabatta roll in half and moisten the cut surfaces with extra virgin olive oil. Layer torn radicchio leaves and two thin slices of fontina cheese on the base, and add some arugula leaves and roasted red bell pepper slices (bought from the deli counter). Add 2 thin slices prosciutto, loosely folded, and season generously. Position the top part of the roll and press down lightly. Heat through, if desired.

pizza dough base

Pizzas were first created in Naples, essentially as street food. Even today, the best pizzas are still made in the south, where local wheat and water produce the finest texture and crust. The best type of flour to use is Italian "0" grade (not the "00" type used for pasta, which isn't suitable).

Basically a pizza is a flat bread, used as a base for toppings that range from the simplest marinara (see right) to many more sophisticated concoctions. In Italy, pizzas are a serious business. There are rules and standards, and every *pizzaiola* (pizza-maker) must possess a licence from the government to ensure that he satisfies these.

MAKES TWO 10-INCH PIZZA BASES

2 cakes (0.6-oz each) compressed fresh yeast, or
  1½ teaspoons quick-rising active dry yeast
2¼ cups all-purpose or white bread flour
½ teaspoon fine sea salt
4 tablespoons olive oil, plus extra for oiling
semolina for sprinkling

1 Measure ¼ cup warm water. Blend the fresh yeast (or simply mix dry yeast) with a little of this water.

2 Sift the flour and salt together into a large bowl. Make a well in the center and add the olive oil, yeast liquid, and some of the remaining water. Mix together with a wooden spoon, gradually adding the rest of the water, to form a soft dough.

3 Turn the dough onto a lightly floured surface and knead vigorously for 10 minutes until it is soft and satiny (don't be afraid to add more flour). Place in a lightly oiled large bowl, then turn the dough around to coat with the oil. Cover the bowl with a clean dish towel and leave in a warm place for 1½ hours, or until the dough has doubled in size.

4 Preheat the oven to 400°F. In the bottom of the oven, heat two oiled baking sheets or a terracotta pizza stone. Punch down the dough with your knuckles, then turn onto a lightly floured surface and knead for 2–3 minutes to knock out the air bubbles. Divide the dough in half.

5 On a lightly floured surface, preferably marble, roll out the pieces of dough very, very thinly, until 10–12 inches in diameter. (They should be as thin as a paper napkin folded in four.) Now lift each pizza base onto a cold baking sheet sprinkled generously with semolina (this will make it easier to slide the pizza off). Add your chosen topping.

6 Lightly oil the preheated baking sheets. Carefully slide the prepared pizzas off the cold baking sheets directly onto the hot baking sheets, or pizza stone, and immediately put into the oven. Bake for 20–25 minutes until golden and crisp.

pizza marinara

This is the original, simple tomato pizza. Purists in Naples claim there are only two authentic pizzas: the marinara and the margarita. I favor the marinara because I love its fresh taste and simplicity. For extra flavor, you might like to scatter some anchovies on top before baking.

SERVES 2

1 recipe of pizza dough (page 70)
4–5 fresh plum tomatoes, peeled
6–8 basil leaves, torn

1 garlic clove, peeled and chopped
1 tablespoon dried oregano
sea salt and freshly ground black pepper
extra virgin olive oil for drizzling

1   Preheat the oven to 400°F, with two baking sheets or a pizza stone inside. On a lightly floured surface, roll out the pizza dough very thinly into two 10- to 12-inch rounds, then lift each pizza base onto a cold baking sheet sprinkled with semolina (see page 70).

2   Put the tomatoes, basil, and seasoning in a blender or food processor and blend to a purée, or pass through a food mill. Spread this tomato sauce over the pizza bases and top with the garlic and oregano.

3   Slide the pizzas onto the oiled hot baking sheets, or pizza stone, and bake for about 20 minutes until the crust is crisp and golden brown. Drizzle with extra virgin olive oil to serve.

pizza margarita

I love simple food: good ingredients, carefully combined and used at their freshest, are a joy. This fresh tomato and mozzarella pizza couldn't be more straightforward. For the best flavor, choose bright red, ripe tomatoes with a distinctive peppery aroma (detected at the stem end).

SERVES 4–6

1 recipe of pizza dough (page 70)
large handful of basil leaves, torn
1½ lb cherry tomatoes, halved

small handful of oregano leaves, chopped
9 oz mozzarella cheese, shredded
sea salt and freshly ground black pepper

1   Preheat the oven to 400°F, with two baking sheets or a pizza stone inside. On a lightly floured surface, roll out the dough very thinly into two 10- to 12-inch rounds. Lift each pizza base onto a cold baking sheet sprinkled with semolina (see page 70).

2   Scatter the basil leaves over the pizza bases, then add the cherry tomato halves, chopped oregano, salt, pepper, and shredded mozzarella.

3   Slide the pizzas onto the oiled hot baking sheets, or pizza stone, and bake for about 20 minutes until the tomatoes are softened and the cheese is bubbling and golden.

pizza with eggplant and ricotta

I love eggplants, and this is one of my favorite ways of eating them. Although not everyone does so, I always salt and rinse eggplants before cooking them. First and foremost, salting draws out beads of bitter juices; and secondly, the eggplants will absorb less oil afterward.
Illustrated on previous page

SERVES 2

1 recipe of pizza dough (page 70)
1 medium eggplant
3 tablespoons olive oil
1 small red onion, peeled and sliced into rings
4 ripe tomatoes, peeled and sliced
¼ cup freshly grated Parmesan cheese
1 cup ricotta cheese
large handful of basil leaves
sea salt and freshly ground black pepper

1   Wrap the pizza dough in plastic wrap and set aside until you are ready to roll out. Slice the eggplant lengthwise, then put the slices into a colander, sprinkle with salt, cover with a plate, and weight down with a can of food. Leave for 30 minutes to drain the bitter juices.

2   Preheat the broiler. If the oven is separate, preheat it to 400°F, with two baking sheets or a pizza stone inside (otherwise, wait until you have broiled the eggplants to heat the oven).

3   Heat one-third of the olive oil in a saucepan, add the onion rings, and fry until softened. Add the tomatoes, salt, and pepper, and set aside.

4   Rinse the eggplant slices to remove the salt and pat dry. Brush them with half the remaining olive oil, then broil for 5 minutes on each side until lightly cooked.

5   On a lightly floured surface, roll out the pizza dough very thinly into two 10- to 12-inch rounds. Lift each pizza base onto a cold baking sheet sprinkled with semolina (see page 70). Brush with the remaining olive oil, then spread with the tomato mixture. Sprinkle on the Parmesan cheese and add the ricotta. Arrange the eggplant slices on top, radiating from the center, then tuck some of the basil leaves under the slices.

6   Slide the pizzas onto the oiled hot baking sheets, or the pizza stone, and bake for 20–25 minutes until golden and bubbling. Serve hot, scattered with the rest of the basil leaves.

pizza norcina

I first enjoyed this pizza in Norcina, in Umbria, a region famous for its truffles. It tasted so good that I returned the following day for another. Truffle-hunting is taken very seriously in Umbria: a good truffle is a real prize and it becomes a talking point for months on end. Here I have used truffle paste, made from a combination of truffle and porcini mushrooms, and available in jars.

SERVES 2

1 recipe of pizza dough (page 70)
1 oz dried porcini mushrooms
9 oz portobello mushrooms, wiped
2 tablespoons olive oil
1 garlic clove, peeled and crushed
9 oz mozzarella cheese, shredded
1 oz truffle paste (salsina)
sea salt and freshly ground black pepper

1   Wrap the pizza dough in plastic wrap and set aside until ready to roll out. Preheat the oven to 400°F with two baking sheets or a pizza stone inside.

2   Soak the dried porcini in warm water to cover for about 20 minutes, then drain and pat dry. Slice the fresh mushrooms.

3   Heat the olive oil in a frying pan, add the porcini and sliced fresh mushrooms, and fry until softened. Add the garlic and some salt and pepper.

4   On a lightly floured surface, roll out the pizza dough very thinly into two 10- to 12-inch rounds. Lift each pizza base onto a cold baking sheet sprinkled with semolina (see page 70). Top the pizza bases with the mushrooms and mozzarella, then add little mounds of truffle paste.

5   Slide the pizzas onto the oiled hot baking sheets, or pizza stone, and bake for 20–25 minutes until golden and bubbling. Serve immediately.

asparagus calzone

To make calzone, you simply fold the pizza dough over the filling and seal the edges, like a turnover. Here, the sweet, succulent flavor and aroma of fresh asparagus is held within, until you cut into the calzone. Make this in early summer, when outdoor-grown asparagus is in season.

SERVES 2

1 recipe of pizza dough (page 70)

2 tender, young zucchini

12 oz asparagus spears

²/₃ cup ricotta cheese

1 tablespoon freshly grated Parmesan cheese

2 tablespoons olive oil

sea salt and freshly ground black pepper

1 Wrap the pizza dough in plastic wrap and set aside until ready to roll out. Preheat the oven to 400°F with a baking sheet or a pizza stone inside. Slice the zucchini, place in a colander, and sprinkle with salt. Let drain for 20 minutes, then rinse under cold water and pat dry.

2 Cut off the pale stalk ends and peel the lower end of the asparagus stalks, using a swivel vegetable peeler. Add the asparagus spears to a saucepan of boiling water and return to a boil, then immediately drain and rinse under cold water. Cut into 2-inch pieces and pat dry.

3 Put the asparagus, zucchini, ricotta, and Parmesan into a bowl. Mix together and season with salt and pepper to taste. Stir in 1 tablespoon olive oil.

4 On a lightly floured surface, roll out the pizza dough into two 10- to 12-inch rounds. Lift each round onto a cold baking sheet sprinkled with semolina (see page 70). Pile the filling on one side of each round, moisten the edge with water, and bring the uncovered side over the filling. Using your fingers, press the edges together to seal, fold them up, and crimp.

5 Brush the calzone with the remaining olive oil, slide onto the hot oiled baking sheet, or pizza stone, and bake for 20–25 minutes until golden brown. Let stand for 10 minutes before serving.

Gorgonzola and artichoke pizza

This versatile pizza can be served hot, straight from the oven, or cold for a picnic. Canned artichokes are a great pantry standby and a convenient alternative to preparing fresh artichoke hearts. For this recipe, I roast them first before arranging on the pizza.

SERVES 2

1 recipe of pizza dough (page 70)

6 canned artichoke hearts

3 tablespoons olive oil

5 oz mozzarella cheese, shredded

5 oz Gorgonzola cheese, sliced

3 tablespoons freshly grated Parmesan cheese

1 tablespoon pine nuts, toasted

1 teaspoon minced sage

sea salt and freshly ground black pepper

1 Wrap the pizza dough in plastic wrap and set aside until ready to roll out. Preheat the oven to 400°F with two baking sheets or a pizza stone inside.

2 Rinse the artichokes well, pat dry, and place in a small roasting pan. Drizzle with the olive oil and roast for 10 minutes until golden. Transfer to a board and cut into quarters.

3 On a lightly floured surface, roll out the pizza dough very thinly into two 10- to 12-inch rounds. Lift each pizza base onto a cold baking sheet sprinkled with semolina (see page 70).

4 Scatter the mozzarella and Gorgonzola over the pizza bases and arrange the artichoke hearts on top. Sprinkle with the Parmesan, pine nuts, and sage, and season with salt and pepper.

5 Slide the pizzas onto the oiled hot baking sheets, or pizza stone, and bake for 20–25 minutes until golden and bubbling. Eat hot or cold.

spinach, olive, and onion testo

I first enjoyed this *testo* in Naples airport. Baked as a large, flat round, the olive-oil-enriched dough has a tasty spinach, mozzarella, and olive filling in the middle. It is cut into wedges to serve, and I like to take it on picnics.

MAKES 1

FOR THE DOUGH:
2 cakes (0.6-oz each) compressed fresh yeast, or
  1½ teaspoons quick-rising active dry yeast
4 cups all-purpose or white bread flour
2 teaspoons fine sea salt
3 tablespoons olive oil

FOR THE FILLING:
2 tablespoons olive oil
1 large red onion, peeled and sliced
1 garlic clove, peeled and crushed
½ dried long, thin, red chili pepper (peperoncini),
  crushed
1¾ lb spinach, trimmed and minced
1 cup pitted green olives
3 oz mozzarella cheese, chopped
sea salt and freshly ground black pepper

TO FINISH:
olive oil for drizzling
coarse sea salt for sprinkling

1 First prepare the dough. Measure 9 fl oz warm water. Mix the yeast with 1 tablespoon of the water. Put the flour and salt into a large bowl and mix well together. Make a well in the middle and pour in the yeast liquid, the olive oil, and some of the remaining water. Mix together, gradually adding the rest of the measured water, to form a soft dough.

2 Turn the dough onto a lightly floured work surface and knead vigorously for 10 minutes until smooth. Return the dough to a clean bowl, cover with a cloth, and leave in a warm place for 45 minutes until doubled in size.

3 Knead the risen dough again for 1–2 minutes to punch out the air bubbles. Return to the bowl, cover, and let rise for about 40 minutes.

4 For the filling, heat the olive oil in a large frying pan. Add the onion, garlic, and chili, and cook for about 5 minutes. Add the spinach and cook for 5 minutes longer until it is wilted. Remove from the heat, add the olives, and season with salt and pepper. Let cool, then mix in the mozzarella.

5 Divide the dough in half. Roll out each piece on a lightly floured surface to a 13-inch round. Place one round on a lightly oiled baking sheet and spoon the filling on top, leaving a margin around the edge. Dampen the edge, cover with the second round of dough, and pinch the edges together to seal. Let rise for 30 minutes. Preheat the oven to 400°F.

6 Drizzle the testo with olive oil and sprinkle with coarse sea salt. Bake for 25 minutes, then transfer to a wire rack. Serve hot, warm, or cold, cut into wedges.

4 pasta, polenta, and rice

parsley pasta with clams and black olives

Linguine and trenette are similar long, thin, ribbon pasta, rather like flattened spaghetti. I like to serve this fine pasta with an unusual clam and olive sauce, inspired by a similar dish that I enjoyed on the Sardinian coast.

SERVES 4

12 oz dried linguine or trenette pasta

very large handful of flat-leaf parsley,
  minced

3 tablespoons extra virgin olive oil

sea salt and freshly ground black pepper

FOR THE CLAM SAUCE:

10 ripe plum tomatoes

2 tablespoons olive oil

3 garlic cloves, peeled and chopped

40 fresh hardshell clams

1 celery stalk, minced

20 Gaeta olives, pitted

3/4 cup dry white wine

handful of basil leaves, roughly torn

1 For the sauce, immerse the tomatoes in a bowl of boiling hot water for 10 seconds to loosen the skins, then drain and peel away the skins. Chop the tomato flesh. Heat the olive oil in a large, heavy-based sauté pan. Add the garlic and sauté over a medium heat until very lightly golden. Add the clams, cover the pan with a tight-fitting lid, and cook over a high heat for 4–6 minutes until the shells have opened. Discard any clams that remain closed.

2 Meanwhile, add the pasta to a large pan of boiling salted water and cook at a fast boil until *al dente* (tender but firm to the bite).

3 Add the tomatoes, celery, olives, and wine to the clams and cook until the wine evaporates, about 1 minute. Season with salt and pepper to taste and scatter in the torn basil. Remove from the heat.

4 Drain the pasta well and toss with the parsley and extra virgin olive oil. Combine with the clam sauce, and eat immediately.

pasta "Norma"

This dish is thought to have been invented by a Sicilian chef, for the first performance of Bellini's opera "Norma" to be performed on the island. It is a typical southern Italian pasta dish—colorful, with robust flavors. When fresh plum tomatoes are out of season, use canned tomatoes; the basil-flavored variety works well here.

SERVES 6

2¼ lb fresh plum tomatoes, or
  28 oz canned crushed tomatoes
5 tablespoons olive oil
1 onion, peeled and minced
2 garlic cloves, peeled and crushed

2 medium eggplants, trimmed
1 lb penne rigate (pasta quills with ridges)
handful of small basil leaves
sea salt and freshly ground black pepper
freshly grated Parmesan cheese for serving

1 If using fresh tomatoes, plunge them into boiling water for 10 seconds, then drain and peel away the skins. Quarter the tomatoes and remove the cores. Heat 2 tablespoons olive oil in a large saucepan, add the onion, and sauté for a few minutes to soften. Add the crushed garlic and sauté for a minute or two, then add the prepared fresh or canned tomatoes and season well with salt and pepper. Cover and cook for 25 minutes.

2 Meanwhile, slice the eggplants lengthwise into strips ¾ inch long. Sprinkle with salt, place in a bowl or colander, cover with a plate, and weight down with a can of food. Leave to drain out the bitter juices for 20 minutes. Rinse the eggplant strips thoroughly and pat dry.

3 Heat the remaining olive oil in a large frying pan, add the eggplant strips, and fry for about 10 minutes, turning frequently, until golden brown on all sides and tender. Drain on paper towels.

4 Bring a large saucepan of salted water to a boil. Add the pasta and cook in fast boiling water until *al dente* (tender but firm to the bite). Drain the pasta and toss with the tomato sauce and eggplant. Scatter with the basil leaves and serve, with plenty of grated Parmesan.

fast pasta sauces

Pasta is the quintessential fast food. Dried pasta cooks in just 10 minutes and can be combined with all manner of tasty sauces to create speedy dishes. It is an ideal choice for a quick supper when you return home from work, hungry and tired.

Look to the wonderful array of Italian ingredients in the supermarket to assemble mouthwatering pasta sauces in a matter of moments. Choose from soft cheeses that melt effortlessly, pots of prepared pesto (red and green), dried chili peppers, preserved artichokes, sun-dried tomatoes, pancetta dice, and baby spinach and arugula leaves that wilt on contact with hot pasta. Select ripe, flavorful fresh tomatoes or use canned crushed tomatoes, and keep a wedge of Parmesan in the fridge, plus some fresh herbs such as parsley and basil.

Each of the following sauces is sufficient to serve 4; you will need to cook about 12 oz dried pasta of your choice.

▲ **garlicky shrimp and tomato sauce**
Peel 8 oz raw tiger shrimp. Heat 3 tbsp olive oil in a sauté pan. Add the shrimp with 2 crushed garlic cloves and 1 seeded and chopped fresh red chili pepper and sauté for 3–4 minutes or until the shrimp turn pink. Add 8 seeded and diced plum tomatoes, along with 2 tbsp chopped flat-leaf parsley and toss to mix. Immediately tip into bowls of freshly cooked hot pasta and serve.

tomato and chili sauce

Cook 4 minced garlic cloves in 2 tbsp olive oil until softened. Add 9 oz baby plum or roma tomatoes and 1–2 seeded and chopped hot red chili peppers (depending on palate). Cook over a gentle heat for about 15 minutes until the tomatoes soften and split. Mix in 2 tbsp each of torn basil leaves and chopped flat-leaf parsley. Season with salt and pepper, and toss with your favorite freshly cooked pasta.

three-cheese sauce

Chop 4 oz each of 3 creamy cheeses, such as ricotta, Dolcelatte or Gorgonzola, and Taleggio. Add to a pan of freshly cooked, hot tagliatelle or other pasta of your choice and toss until melted into an instant creamy sauce. Divide among warm bowls and sprinkle with about 4 tbsp chopped flat-leaf parsley, plenty of freshly grated Parmesan, and a generous grinding of black pepper. Serve immediately.

▲ creamy chicken and mushroom sauce

Buy a large cooked chicken breast half, remove the skin, and chop the meat into pieces. Sauté 4 oz sliced button, oyster, or cremini mushrooms in 3 tbsp olive oil until softened. Add the chopped chicken, 2/3 cup dry white wine, 4 tbsp light cream, 2 tbsp minced rosemary leaves, and some salt and pepper. Cook, stirring occasionally, for 5 minutes, then serve with your favorite freshly cooked pasta.

pumpkin ravioli

These small, plump pasta circles are filled with pumpkin and crumbled amaretti cookies, and served drizzled with a fragrant sage butter. The recipe is a specialty of Mantua, a beautiful city that boasts an impressive ducal palace with wonderful frescoes by Mantegna.
Illustrated on previous page

SERVES 6

FOR THE PASTA:
2$^{1}/_{2}$ cups Italian "00" flour
$^{3}/_{4}$ teaspoon fine sea salt
3 eggs

FOR THE STUFFING AND SAGE BUTTER:
1 small pumpkin, about 2$^{1}/_{4}$ lb
2 garlic cloves, peeled and crushed
6 amaretti cookies, finely crumbled
1 cup freshly grated Parmesan cheese
6 tablespoons unsalted butter
handful of sage leaves
sea salt and freshly ground black pepper

1 Preheat the oven to 350°F. To make the stuffing, cut the pumpkin into large pieces using a sharp knife, and discard the seeds and fibers. Place the pumpkin on a foil-lined baking sheet and bake for 30 minutes. Let cool, then remove the skin. Put the pumpkin flesh into a food processor with the garlic and seasoning, and blend to a purée. Mix the pumpkin purée with the crumbled amaretti and half of the Parmesan. Check the seasoning.

2 To make the pasta, heap the flour into a mound on a board and sprinkle with the salt. Make a well in the center. Break the eggs into the well and gradually work them into the flour to form a dough. Knead until smooth and elastic.

3 Divide the pasta dough in half and roll out into two very thin sheets of equal size, using a pasta machine if possible. Place small mounds of the pumpkin mixture on one pasta sheet, spacing them about 2 inches apart. Top with the second pasta sheet and press lightly around each mound of filling to seal. Cut out the ravioli, using a fluted 2-inch round cutter.

4 Bring a large saucepan of salted water to a boil. Drop in the ravioli and cook until *al dente* (tender but firm to the bite), about 2–3 minutes. Meanwhile, melt the butter in a small saucepan and add the sage leaves.

5 Drain the ravioli and divide among warm plates. Sprinkle with the remaining Parmesan and drizzle with the sage butter. Eat at once.

pansôti with walnut sauce

Triangles of fresh pasta are stuffed with a tasty mixture of fresh herbs, garlic, and ricotta, and served with a creamy walnut sauce. This recipe is popular all along the Ligurian coastline and it takes its name, pansôti, from the regional name for ravioli. The walnut sauce, which can be made in advance, is often referred to as "winter pesto."

SERVES 6

FOR THE PASTA:

2 cups Italian "00" flour

$^1/_2$ teaspoon fine sea salt

2 eggs

FOR THE FILLING AND SAUCE:

1 cup chopped chervil

1 cup chopped chives

1 cup chopped marjoram

2 garlic cloves

1 egg

6 tablespoons ricotta cheese

$2^1/_2$ cups slightly dry, coarse bread crumbs, soaked in water and squeezed dry

1 cup walnut halves

1 cup freshly grated Parmesan cheese

$^1/_2$ cup heavy cream

4 tablespoons extra virgin olive oil

sea salt and freshly ground black pepper

1 To make the pasta, heap the flour in a mound on a board, sprinkle with the salt, and make a well in the center. Break the eggs into the well and gradually work them into the flour, adding sufficient water to make a soft dough. Knead until smooth and elastic. Wrap in plastic wrap and chill for 20 minutes.

2 For the filling, mix the chopped herbs, garlic, egg, and ricotta together in a bowl and add half of the soaked bread crumbs. Mix well, seasoning with salt and pepper to taste.

3 Blanch the walnuts in boiling water for 1 minute, then drain and peel off the skins. Place the nuts in a blender with the remaining soaked bread crumbs, 1 tablespoon Parmesan, the cream, and olive oil. Blend to a creamy consistency. Transfer the sauce to a small saucepan and warm gently.

4 Roll out the pasta dough, using a pasta machine, to the second thinnest setting. Cut into 2½-inch squares. Place a small amount of filling in the center of each square and fold the dough back over to form a triangle, pressing the edges together lightly to seal in the filling.

5 Cook the pansôti in plenty of boiling salted water until *al dente* (tender but firm to the bite), about 3 minutes. Drain and serve topped with the walnut sauce and remaining Parmesan.

pasta with meatballs in tomato sauce

This is a classic dish from Campania, my home region. Ground beef, veal, and pork are made into meatballs and cooked in a rich tomato sauce, to be served with pasta. Conveniently, both the sauce and meatballs can be made in advance.

SERVES 6

FOR THE MEATBALLS:
9 oz (about 1 cup) lean ground beef
9 oz (about 1 cup) lean ground veal
4 oz (about 1/2 cup) lean ground pork
handful of flat-leaf parsley, minced
1/2 teaspoon oregano leaves, minced
2 tablespoons dry vermouth
grated zest of 2 lemons

2 cups soft, white bread crumbs
2 eggs
2 garlic cloves, peeled and crushed
sea salt and freshly ground black pepper

FOR THE SAUCE AND PASTA:
3 cups bottled tomato passata (purée)
14 oz penne, cellentani, or macaroni

FOR SERVING:
Parmesan cheese shavings

1 First, prepare the meatballs: Combine all the ingredients in a bowl and season generously with salt and pepper. Mix thoroughly with a wooden spoon until evenly blended. Shape into small balls about 3/4 inch in diameter.

2 Pour the passata into a large, shallow pan. Bring to a simmer and add the meatballs. Cover and cook over a medium heat for 40 minutes.

3 Toward the end of the cooking time, add the pasta to a large pan of boiling salted water and cook at a fast boil until *al dente* (tender but firm to the bite). Drain well.

4 Divide the hot pasta among warm bowls and pour the meatballs in tomato sauce over the top. Toss to mix, sprinkle with Parmesan shavings, and serve at once.

spaghetti with Italian sausage

Enjoyed throughout the whole of Italy, but originating from the Marches, this is a great favorite with children. It is one of the easiest of the classic pasta dishes to prepare.

SERVES 6

12 oz spaghetti
sea salt and freshly ground black pepper

FOR THE SAUCE:
1³/₄ lb Italian sausage
2 tablespoons olive oil
1 onion, peeled and minced
1 teaspoon oregano leaves
3 cups bottled tomato passata (purée)
1 bay leaf
2 tablespoons dry vermouth

FOR SERVING:
handful of flat-leaf parsley, minced

1 First prepare the sauce. Cut the sausage into 1-inch pieces and place in a shallow pan with 6 tablespoons water. Bring to a simmer and cook until the water has evaporated.

2 Heat the olive oil in another pan, add the onion, and sauté for about 5 minutes until soft. Add the sausage and oregano, and cook for 5 minutes longer. Add the tomato passata, bay leaf, and vermouth, and simmer uncovered for 30 minutes. Season with salt and pepper to taste.

3 Toward the end of the cooking time, add the spaghetti to a large pan of boiling salted water and cook at a fast boil until *al dente* (tender but firm to the bite), about 8–10 minutes. Drain well.

4 Divide the spaghetti among warm plates and pour the hot sauce over the top. Sprinkle with parsley and serve.

lasagne with chicken

Lasagne is always popular and it's an ideal dish for a family meal or informal party, not least because it can be made ahead of time. As a change from the familiar beef filling, this version—known as *lasagne alla cacciatore* in Italy—features chicken and mushrooms.

SERVES 6–8

9 oz dried egg lasagne (requiring no
   pre-cooking)

FOR THE FILLING:
6 chicken breast halves
2 tablespoons olive oil
2 rosemary sprigs, leaves only, chopped
1 onion, peeled and minced
3/4 cup white wine
28 oz canned crushed tomatoes
6 tablespoons unsalted butter

2 garlic cloves, peeled and crushed
1 lb cremini mushrooms
handful of flat-leaf parsley, minced
handful of basil leaves, torn
sea salt and freshly ground black pepper

FOR THE SAUCE:
6 tablespoons unsalted butter
3/4 cup Italian "00" flour
2 1/2 cups milk, warmed
1/2 cup freshly grated Parmesan cheese, plus
   extra for serving (optional)

1 Preheat the oven to 400°F. For the filling, season the chicken breasts, rub with a little olive oil, place in a roasting pan, and sprinkle with the rosemary. Roast for 20 minutes.

2 Meanwhile, heat the remaining olive oil in a saucepan, add the onion, and cook for 5 minutes or until softened and golden. Add the wine and let it evaporate. Next, add the crushed tomatoes and bring to a simmer. Season with salt and pepper, and simmer for 20 minutes.

3 In the meantime, heat the butter in a frying pan. Add the garlic and mushrooms, and sauté until golden, turning once. Season with salt and pepper. Add the mushrooms to the tomatoes, along with the chopped parsley and basil.

4 Cut the cooked chicken breasts into strips and add to the mushroom and tomato mixture. Adjust the seasoning and set aside. Lower the oven setting to 350°F.

5 To make the sauce, melt the butter in a heavy-based saucepan, stir in the flour, and cook for 1–2 minutes until golden. Add the warmed milk little by little to form a thick sauce, stirring over a medium heat until thick and smooth. Stir in half of the Parmesan and season to taste. (Unless you are assembling the dish right away, cover the surface with a damp piece of parchment paper to prevent a skin from forming.)

6 Line a lasagne dish with a layer of sauce, then cover with a layer of lasagne sheets. Spoon half of the chicken and mushroom mixture on top, then add another layer of lasagne. Cover with the remaining chicken and mushroom mixture and a final layer of lasagne. Spread the rest of the sauce on top and sprinkle with the remaining Parmesan. Bake for 25 minutes until golden and bubbling. Serve with extra grated Parmesan, if required.

polenta with wild mushrooms

Here, a basic polenta is left to set, then cut into wedges, pan-grilled, and served topped with a wild mushroom sauce. It makes an elegant *primi piatti* (first course) for a special dinner.

SERVES 4

FOR THE POLENTA:

1³/₄ cups coarse polenta (cornmeal)

4 tablespoons unsalted butter, cut into cubes

¹/₂ cup freshly grated Parmesan cheese

sea salt and freshly ground black pepper

FOR THE MUSHROOM SAUCE:

1¹/₂ lb wild or cultivated open-cap mushrooms

4 tablespoons olive oil

1 small garlic clove, peeled and crushed

1 tablespoon chopped thyme, plus a few sprigs

²/₃ cup white wine

2 tablespoons chopped flat-leaf parsley

1 Bring 7¹/₂ cups water to a boil in a large saucepan with 1 teaspoon salt added. Gradually add the polenta, letting it run through your fingers in a thin stream, and stirring constantly to prevent lumps. Simmer for 35 minutes, until the mixture comes away from the sides of the pan, stirring often.

2 When the polenta is cooked, stir in the butter, Parmesan, and pepper to taste. (At this stage, you have what is known as "wet polenta," which can be served as a simple accompaniment.)

3 While the polenta is still hot, spread it out on a dampened baking sheet or wooden board, to ¹/₂-inch thickness. Leave for about 1 hour until softly set.

4 Meanwhile, make the sauce. Halve or quarter any large mushrooms. Heat the olive oil and garlic in a pan, then add the mushrooms and thyme, and cook over a high heat for 1 minute. Season with salt and pepper. Add the wine and boil vigorously until almost totally evaporated. Stir in the parsley.

5 Preheat a ridged grill pan or the broiler. Cut the polenta into triangles and pan-grill or broil on both sides until lightly charred. Serve on warm plates, topped with the mushroom sauce and thyme sprigs.

fried polenta sandwiches

Similar to the more familiar *mozzarella in carrozza*, this is a delicious way of using up leftover polenta. If you are unable to find fontina, you can use mozzarella cheese instead. A popular snack, with children and adults.

MAKES 6

FOR THE POLENTA:
2¹/₂ cups vegetable broth (page 47)
    or water
1 cup coarse polenta (cornmeal)
¹/₄ cup freshly grated Parmesan cheese
2 tablespoons unsalted butter
sea salt and freshly ground black pepper

TO ASSEMBLE AND COOK:
4 oz fontina cheese
6 slices of prosciutto
flour for dusting
1 egg, beaten
4 cups fresh white bread crumbs
olive oil for shallow-frying

1 Pour the vegetable broth or water into a large saucepan, add ¹/₂ teaspoon salt, and bring to a boil. Gradually add the polenta, letting it run through your fingers in a thin stream, and stirring constantly to prevent lumps from forming. Simmer for 30 minutes, until the mixture comes away from the sides of the pan, stirring frequently.

2 When the polenta is cooked, stir in the Parmesan, butter, and some pepper. Spread the hot polenta mixture on a dampened baking sheet or wooden board, to ¹/₂-inch thickness. Leave for about 1 hour until set.

3 Cut the set polenta into rounds, using a 3-inch cutter. Slice the fontina cheese to the same size as the polenta rounds. Sandwich a slice of cheese and a piece of prosciutto between two rounds of polenta. Press well together.

4 Dust the polenta sandwiches with flour to coat all over, then dip into the beaten egg and, finally, into the bread crumbs. Press lightly, so the bread crumbs adhere.

5 Heat the olive oil in a large frying pan and shallow-fry the polenta sandwiches on both sides until golden brown. Drain on paper towels, then serve hot.

rice balls

Enjoyed throughout Italy, these cheesy rice balls are known as *supplì di riso*, or *supplì al telefono* because the mozzarella stretches like telephone wires as they are eaten. Ideal party food or antipasto, they are a good way of using leftover risotto, though here the risotto is freshly made.

SERVES 4

3½ cups vegetable broth (page 47)

4 tablespoons unsalted butter

1¼ cups risotto rice (such as vialone nano, carnaroli, or arborio)

6 oz mozzarella cheese, cut into small cubes

6 shallots, peeled and minced

finely grated zest of 1 large orange

handful of mixed herbs (such as flat-leaf parsley, basil, and oregano), chopped

6 tablespoons freshly grated Parmesan cheese

sea salt and freshly ground black pepper

TO ASSEMBLE AND COOK:

1 egg, lightly beaten

1 heaped cup fresh white bread crumbs

6 tablespoons olive oil

1 Heat the broth in a saucepan until almost boiling, then reduce the heat and keep at a low simmer.

2 Heat the butter in a wide, heavy-based saucepan. Add the rice and stir, using a wooden spoon, until the grains are well coated and glistening, about 1 minute. Add a ladleful of hot broth and simmer, stirring, until it has been absorbed. Continue to add the broth at intervals and cook as before, until all the liquid has been absorbed and the rice is *al dente* (tender but retaining a bite), about 18–20 minutes.

3 Add the mozzarella, shallots, orange zest, mixed herbs, Parmesan, and salt and pepper to taste. Mix well. Remove from the heat and let cool. (The rice is easier to handle and shape when it is cold.)

4 Using your hands, shape the rice mixture into 8 balls. Dip each one into the beaten egg and coat well, then roll in the bread crumbs to coat. Use your fingers to press crumbs onto any uncoated surface.

5 Heat the olive oil in a frying pan. Fry the rice balls, in batches if necessary, until golden on all sides, about 8 minutes. Drain well on paper towels. Serve hot or cold.

saffron risotto

This classic *risotto alla milanese* is a specialty of Lombardy. I use saffron threads rather than the powdered form, which tends to be of a lesser quality and flavor. My sisters often make this dish as their children adore it—they call it "happy food" because of its bright yellow color.

SERVES 4

3¾ cups vegetable broth (page 47)
4 tablespoons unsalted butter
1 tablespoon olive oil
8 shallots, peeled and minced
½ teaspoon saffron threads
1¼ cups risotto rice (such as vialone nano,
   carnaroli, or arborio)

about ⅓ cup white wine
1 cup freshly grated Parmesan cheese,
   plus extra for serving
2 tablespoons light cream
handful of flat-leaf parsley, coarsely chopped
   (optional)
sea salt and freshly ground black pepper

1 Heat the broth in a saucepan until almost boiling, then reduce the heat and keep at a low simmer.

2 Heat the butter and olive oil in a wide, heavy-based saucepan over a medium heat. Add the shallots and cook for 1–2 minutes, until softened but not browned. Add the saffron and stir until its yellow color is released, then add the rice. Stir with a wooden spoon until the rice grains are well coated and glistening, about 1 minute.

3 Add the wine and stir until absorbed. Add a ladleful of hot broth and simmer, stirring, until it has been absorbed. Continue to add the broth at intervals and cook as before, until the liquid is absorbed and the rice is *al dente* (tender but retaining a bite), 18–20 minutes. Save the last ladleful of broth.

4 Add the Parmesan, cream, reserved broth, chopped parsley, if using, and some salt and pepper. Stir well, then remove from the heat. Cover and let rest for 2 minutes. Spoon into warm bowls and serve with extra Parmesan.

tomato risotto

The simplicity of this dish appeals to me and probably accounts for its popularity with children as well as grown-ups. It's almost impossible to imagine Italian food without tomatoes. Use a full-flavored variety—firm, red, and with a good fruity scent.

SERVES 4

4 cups vegetable broth (page 47)

4 tablespoons unsalted butter

1 tablespoon olive oil

8 shallots, peeled and minced

2 garlic cloves, peeled and crushed

1¼ cups risotto rice (such as vialone nano, carnaroli, or arborio)

about ⅓ cup white wine

8 firm, ripe tomatoes, seeded and coarsely chopped

1 cup freshly grated Parmesan cheese, plus extra for serving (optional)

2 large handfuls of basil leaves, torn

sea salt and freshly ground black pepper

1 Put the vegetable broth into a saucepan. Heat until almost boiling, then reduce the heat until barely simmering to keep it hot.

2 Heat the butter and olive oil in a wide, heavy-based saucepan over a medium heat. Add the shallots and cook for 1–2 minutes, until softened but not browned. Add the garlic and mix well.

3 Add the rice and stir, using a wooden spoon, until the grains are well coated and glistening, about 1 minute. Pour in the wine and stir until it has been completely absorbed.

4 Add a ladleful of hot broth and simmer, stirring, until it has been absorbed. Continue to add the broth in this way, then, after 10 minutes, add the tomatoes. Add the rest of the broth at intervals and cook as before, for a further 8–10 minutes, until the liquid has been absorbed and the rice is *al dente* (tender but retaining a bite). Reserve the last ladleful of broth.

5 Stir in the Parmesan, reserved broth, half of the basil, and some salt and pepper. Remove from the heat, cover, and let rest for 2 minutes. Spoon into warm bowls, sprinkle with grated Parmesan, if using, and the remaining basil, and serve.

risotto with asparagus, peas, and basil

One of my all-time favorite risottos. So light, fresh, and vibrantly green, it reminds me of early summer, when asparagus and peas grow in abundance. Do make the most of vegetables when they are in season, to enjoy them at their finest and sweetest.

SERVES 4

4 cups vegetable broth (page 47)

4 tablespoons unsalted butter

1 tablespoon olive oil

8 shallots, peeled and minced

1¼ cups risotto rice (such as vialone nano, carnaroli, or arborio)

about ⅓ cup white wine

1 cup shelled fresh or frozen, thawed green peas

12 oz asparagus spears, cut into 1½-inch lengths

finely grated zest of 1 lemon

1 cup freshly grated Parmesan cheese

large handful of basil leaves, torn

sea salt and freshly ground black pepper

FOR SERVING (OPTIONAL):

handful of basil leaves, torn

freshly grated Parmesan cheese

1   Put the vegetable broth into a saucepan. Heat until almost boiling, then reduce the heat until barely simmering to keep it hot.

2   Heat the butter and olive oil in a wide, heavy-based saucepan over a medium heat. Add the shallots and cook for 1–2 minutes, until softened but not browned.

3   Add the rice and stir, using a wooden spoon, until the grains are well coated and glistening, about 1 minute. Pour in the wine and stir until completely absorbed.

4   Add a ladleful of hot broth and simmer, stirring, until it has been absorbed. Continue to add the broth in this way, then, after 10 minutes, add the fresh peas, if using, asparagus, and lemon zest and mix well. Continue to add the broth at intervals and cook as before, for a further 8–10 minutes, until the liquid has been absorbed and the rice is *al dente* (tender but retaining a bite). Reserve the last ladleful of broth. If using frozen peas, add 2 minutes before the end of cooking.

5   Add the Parmesan, reserved broth, basil, and some salt and pepper. Mix well. Remove from the heat, cover, and let rest for 2 minutes. Spoon into warm bowls and top with more basil and grated Parmesan, if using. Serve immediately.

5 fish and shellfish

shrimp and white beans Venetian style

The Venetians love seafood and always cook it very carefully. The combination of shrimp and beans in this delicate salad is delicious, and the textures are diverse. It is a simple recipe—just remember to put the cannellini beans to soak the evening before.

SERVES 4

2/3 cup dried cannellini beans, soaked in cold
  water overnight
2 rosemary sprigs
3 bay leaves
3 thyme sprigs
3 flat-leaf parsley sprigs
4 garlic cloves, unpeeled
1 lb large raw shrimp in shell
2 celery stalks, minced
juice of 1 lemon
handful of flat-leaf parsley, chopped
2–3 tablespoons extra virgin olive oil
sea salt and freshly ground black pepper
lemon wedges for serving

1 Drain the cannellini beans and place in a large pan. Add plenty of cold water to cover, plus the herbs and unpeeled garlic. Bring to a boil, then reduce the heat and cook for about 1½ hours or until the beans are tender. Drain the beans and discard the herbs and garlic.

2 Add the shrimp to a pan of boiling salted water and simmer for 2 minutes or until they just turn pink. Immediately drain, peel, and devein them.

3 Combine the beans and shrimp in a bowl and add the celery, lemon juice, and parsley. Season well with salt and pepper, drizzle with the extra virgin olive oil, and toss to mix. Serve with lemon wedges.

fritto misto

This dish of mixed fried fish is very popular throughout Italy. In my native Campania, it is usually made of tiny squid, cuttlefish rings, and scampi (lobsterettes), dusted with flour before being deep-fried in olive oil. It is served crisp and piping hot, with lemon wedges.

SERVES 6

12 oz squid

12 oz lobsterette tails or large raw shrimp
  in shell

12 oz monkfish fillet, skinned

1 cup Italian "00" flour for coating

oil for deep-frying

sea salt

lemon wedges for serving

1 To clean whole squid, pull the pouch and tentacles apart and remove the transparent quill from the pouch. Cut the tentacles away from the head just below the eyes and discard the head, reserving the tentacles. Peel off the transparent outer skin covering the pouch, then cut into rings. Baby squid can simply be halved.

2 If using shrimp, peel away the shell, leaving the tail end intact if you like, and devein.

3 Cut the monkfish into cubes. Wash all the seafood and dry it well on paper towels. Scatter the flour on a board or tray and toss the seafood in it to coat each piece thoroughly.

4 Heat the oil in a deep-fat fryer or deep, heavy-based saucepan to 375°F, or until a cube of bread dropped in browns in 30 seconds. Deep-fry the seafood, a few pieces at a time, until golden and cooked through, about 2–3 minutes.

5 Drain on paper towels, sprinkle with salt, and serve at once accompanied by lemon wedges.

red mullet in an envelope

Baking red mullet in sealed parchment parcels is an excellent way of retaining their delicate flavor and enticing aroma as they cook. The flavor is further enhanced by topping the fish with a piquant anchovy butter before baking. Ask your fishmonger to clean the fish, leaving the liver in if possible, as this adds to the flavor. If you cannot find red mullet, you can substitute other small fish with firm, white flesh.

Illustrated on previous page

SERVES 4

4 red mullet, each about 7 oz, cleaned
4 herb fennel sprigs
large handful of basil leaves
large handful of rosemary leaves
2 tablespoons olive oil
sea salt and freshly ground black pepper

FOR THE ANCHOVY BUTTER:
½ cup (1 stick) unsalted butter, softened
6–8 anchovy fillets in oil, drained

1   Preheat the oven to 425°F. For the anchovy butter, put the softened butter into a bowl, add the anchovy fillets, and mash together using a fork. Chill until ready to use.

2   Rinse and dry the fish well, and put some of the herbs into each cavity. Cut 4 large rectangles of parchment paper (large enough to envelop the fish). Brush the red mullet with olive oil, then place a fish in the center of each parchment rectangle.

3   Sprinkle more herbs on top of the fish and season with salt and pepper. Bring the long edges of the paper up over the fish and fold together firmly. Twist the ends of the paper to seal. Place the packages on a baking sheet and bake for 15–20 minutes.

4   Serve the fish in their fragrant packages, to be opened at the table.

trout with parsley and lemon cream sauce

Trout are to be found in abundance in the rivers of the mountainous Trentino area in the north, which borders Austria. This freshwater fish is best cooked soon after purchase in a light broth. Here, it is served with a lemon and parsley cream sauce.

SERVES 4

4 trout, each about 8 oz, cleaned
5 cups fish broth (page 46) or
  vegetable broth (page 47)
sea salt and freshly ground black pepper

FOR THE SAUCE:
4 tablespoons unsalted butter
1 cup heavy cream
juice of 2 lemons

FOR GARNISH:
handful of flat-leaf parsley, minced

1 Rinse the trout inside and out. Bring the fish or vegetable broth to a boil in a wide, shallow pan. Place the trout in the broth and poach gently just until the flesh is opaque and the eyes are white, about 10 minutes. Lift out and drain well.

2 Meanwhile, make the sauce. Melt the butter in a small saucepan, then add the cream, lemon juice, and some salt. Bring to a simmer, stirring constantly, and simmer for about 5 minutes until reduced. Taste and adjust the seasoning.

3 Place the trout on warm plates. Pour the sauce over the fish, then scatter generously with chopped parsley and serve at once.

stuffed sardines

Sardines are stuffed in many different ways all around the Italian coast. The rosemary and garlic in this dish identify it as Venetian. It takes a little while to prepare sardines for stuffing, but the technique is really not difficult.

SERVES 4

1³/₄ lb fresh sardines, cleaned

¹/₃ cup white bread crumbs (slightly dry)

1 tablespoon chopped rosemary leaves, plus an
    extra stem

2 tablespoons chopped flat-leaf parsley

2 garlic cloves, peeled and minced

6 tablespoons olive oil

juice of 2 lemons

sea salt and freshly ground black pepper

1 Preheat the oven to 400°F. Cut off the heads from the sardines. Slit down the underside, open out the fish, and place flesh-side down on a board. Press down along the spine to flatten and loosen the backbone, then turn over and remove the bone. Wash the fish and pat dry thoroughly.

2 For the stuffing, put the bread crumbs, rosemary, parsley, garlic, and some salt and pepper into a bowl. Pour in 4 tablespoons of the olive oil and mix thoroughly.

3 With the open sardines skin-side down, divide the stuffing among them, spreading it along the middle of each fish. Fold the sides together, so the sardines resume their original shape.

4 Place the sardines, side by side, in a lightly oiled roasting pan in which they fit snugly in a single layer. Sprinkle with salt and pepper. Drizzle with the remaining olive oil and the lemon juice, and lay the rosemary stem on top (for extra flavor). Bake for about 15 minutes until the fish are cooked and a little crisp on top. Serve warm.

marinated fish

Fish is highly valued in Italy, and it is eaten regularly—not surprisingly, considering the extensive 1,500 miles of Italian coastline. Every region has its own special fish dishes, from the fritto misto and fish soups of Calabria in the south, to the marinated fish dishes typical of middle Italy, and seafood dishes of Veneto in the northwest.

Fish cooks quickly, and in Italy it is cooked very simply. Whole fish, steaks, and fillets generally benefit from marinating first, especially if they are to be broiled, grilled, pan-grilled, or roasted in the oven. An oil-based marinade helps to prevent tender fish from becoming dry during cooking. Olive oil is the usual basis, with additional flavorings to suit the particular fish— perhaps a hint of lemon juice and/or zest, balsamic vinegar, a pinch of chili pepper, minced shallots, and a handful of minced herbs. Try the following recipes, varying the flavorings to taste.

▲ **swordfish steaks with capers and anchovies**
To serve 4, place 4 swordfish steaks, each about 8 oz, in a dish in a single layer. Mix 6 tbsp olive oil with 3 tbsp dry white wine, 2 minced shallots, 1 tbsp rinsed small capers, 4 drained, chopped anchovies in oil, and the juice of 1 lemon. Let marinate for 1 hour, then remove. Grill or broil for 6 minutes on each side, depending on thickness, basting occasionally with the marinade.

monkfish spiedini

To serve 4, ask the fishmonger to fillet and skin a 2¹/₄-lb monkfish tail. Cut into 1-inch cubes. Mix the juice of 2 lemons with 2 minced garlic cloves, 1 seeded and chopped hot red chili pepper, 1–2 tsp minced rosemary leaves, and 4 tbsp olive oil. Pour this over the fish and let marinate for 1 hour. Thread the monkfish onto 4 or 8 skewers. Grill or broil for a maximum of 6 minutes, turning once.

grilled marinated sardines

For an antipasto to serve 4, clean and remove the heads from 8 sardines. Place in a dish. Mix 6 tbsp olive oil with 2 tbsp white wine vinegar, 2 crushed garlic cloves, 1 seeded and chopped hot red chili pepper, and 2 tbsp minced parsley. Pour this over the sardines and let marinate for 1 hour, turning once. Remove the sardines from the marinade and grill or broil for 12 minutes, turning once and basting occasionally with the marinade.

▲ sea bass fillets with lemon and chili

To serve 4, place 4 sea bass fillets, each about 7 oz, skin-side down in a shallow baking dish. In a bowl, combine the finely grated zest and juice of 2 lemons, 4 tbsp olive oil, 1 seeded and minced hot red chili pepper, 1 minced garlic clove, and a finely sliced red onion. Pour this over the fish, cover, and let marinate in a cool place for 1 hour. Season the fish and bake at 400°F for 15 minutes or until just tender. Serve at once.

whole fish baked in tomato sauce

Baking a whole fish in a sauce of onions, wine, tomato, and celery is an excellent way of keeping the fish succulent, while imparting extra flavor at the same time. You can use any suitable sized whole white fish. Try, for instance, sea bass, hake, or haddock. Ask your fishmonger to bone the fish, keeping it whole.

SERVES 4

1 whole white fish, about 3 lb, cleaned and
  boned
1–2 tablespoons olive oil
sea salt and freshly ground black pepper

FOR THE SAUCE:
4 tablespoons olive oil
1 medium onion, peeled and minced
1 small celery stalk, minced
1 garlic clove, peeled and minced
1 tablespoon chopped flat-leaf parsley
8 tomatoes, peeled and coarsely chopped
2/3 cup dry white wine

1   Preheat the oven to 400°F. Wash the fish and pat dry, then season with salt inside and out. Place in an oiled roasting pan and brush the skin with olive oil.

2   For the sauce, heat the olive oil in a pan, add the onion, celery, garlic, and parsley, and sauté until the vegetables are soft. Add the tomatoes and wine, and cook for 10 minutes. Season with salt and pepper to taste.

3   Spoon the sauce over and around the fish. Cover the pan with foil and bake for about 30 minutes until the fish is cooked. To test, insert a knife into the thickest part of the body and lift out a little of the flesh—it should be opaque but still moist.

4   Carefully transfer the fish to a warm serving platter and spoon the sauce around. Serve at once.

stuffed sole in saffron sauce

Saffron has always been a feature of Venetian cooking. In times past, this exotic spice was viewed as a sign of wealth, as it gave food the coveted color of real gold. It has a distinctive, complex flavor and must be measured accurately—too much could truly ruin a dish. Get your fishmonger to fillet the fish, and remember to ask for the bones to make the broth.

SERVES 6

3 Dover soles, filleted
2 tablespoons golden raisins
4 oz young, tender spinach leaves,
  stems removed (about 1 heaped cup)
2 tablespoons pine nuts
2 shallots, peeled and minced
2$^{1}/_{2}$ cups fish broth (page 46)
20 saffron threads
$^{1}/_{2}$ cup dry white wine
3 tablespoons unsalted butter, cut into small
  pieces
sea salt and freshly ground black pepper

1   Rinse the sole fillets and pat dry. Put the raisins into a bowl, add 3–4 tablespoons hot water, and leave for 10 minutes to plump up. Drain and pat dry with paper towels.

2   Season the sole fillets with salt and pepper on both sides. Lay the spinach leaves overlapping on each fillet and place some raisins, pine nuts, and minced shallot on top. Roll up the fillets and secure them with string or wooden toothpicks.

3   Bring the fish broth to a boil in a wide, shallow pan. Turn the heat down, then add the fish bundles and cover the pan. Poach gently, with the liquid barely simmering, for 6 minutes.

4   Meanwhile put the saffron threads into a small mortar and pound with the pestle until crushed. Add a tablespoon or two of the hot fish liquid to dissolve the mixture.

5   Using a slotted spoon, remove the sole bundles from the fish broth and place on a warm plate; keep hot. Pour off half of the broth. Add the saffron mixture and wine to the remaining broth in the pan and boil to reduce by half over a high heat. Stir in the pieces of butter, a few at a time.

6   When all the butter has been incorporated, taste and adjust the seasoning. Spoon the sauce around the sole bundles and serve.

roasted monkfish with garlic

Monkfish has a meaty texture and its flavor is exquisite, but it is quite expensive. This is an impressive dish for a dinner party, best served with a simple accompaniment, such as broiled tomatoes. If you're not keen on fennel seeds, simply omit them. Ask your fishmonger to skin and fillet the monkfish by removing the central bone to give two meaty fillets.

SERVES 4

2¹/₄-lb monkfish tail, filleted and skinned
1 large garlic bulb, as fresh as possible
4–5 bay leaves
4 tablespoons olive oil
1 teaspoon thyme leaves
¹/₂ teaspoon fennel seeds (optional)
juice of 1 lemon
sea salt and freshly ground black pepper

1 Preheat the oven to 400°F. Remove all traces of the thin, gray membrane covering the monkfish, then rinse and dry the fish. To hold the fillets together, tie a length of string around the length of the fish, then secure with string at intervals (as shown).

2 Peel 2 garlic cloves from the bulb and cut them into thin slices. Make some incisions in the fish and push in the garlic slices. Tuck the bay leaves under the string.

3 Preheat a shallow roasting pan in the oven for a few minutes. Add half of the olive oil, then lay the fish on the hot pan and turn carefully to coat with the hot oil. Season with salt and pepper, and scatter with the thyme leaves and fennel seeds, if using. Drizzle the lemon juice and remaining olive oil over the fish and surround with the rest of the unpeeled garlic cloves.

4 Roast for 20–30 minutes, basting frequently. Serve with broiled tomatoes, if you like.

tuna steaks with capers

Fine quality swordfish and tuna are caught off the Sicilian coast and this is a specialty of the island. The fish steaks are marinated in white wine with rosemary and garlic, then grilled and served with a sauce of capers and lemon—both found in abundance in Sicily.

SERVES 4

4 tuna or swordfish steaks, each about
  8 oz
1 cup dry white wine
1 rosemary sprig, minced
4 garlic cloves, peeled and minced
olive oil for brushing
2 tablespoons day-old white bread crumbs,
  lightly toasted
sea salt and freshly ground black pepper

FOR THE DRESSING:

4 tablespoons extra virgin olive oil
finely grated zest and juice of 1 lemon
1 tablespoon salted capers, soaked in cold water
  for 20 minutes and drained

1   Place the fish steaks in a shallow dish and season with salt and pepper. Add the wine, rosemary, and garlic, and turn the steaks to coat all over. Let marinate for at least an hour.

2   Drain the fish and pat dry, reserving the marinade. Heat a ridged cast-iron grill pan, or preheat the broiler. Brush the grill (or broiler) pan with olive oil. Cook the fish steaks for 6–8 minutes on each side, depending on thickness, basting frequently with the reserved marinade.

3   Meanwhile, make the dressing: In a small bowl, whisk the olive oil with the lemon juice and zest, capers, and some salt and pepper.

4   Sprinkle the cooked tuna or swordfish with the toasted bread crumbs. Place on warm plates and drizzle with the dressing. Serve with a mixed leaf salad.

tuna and spinach pie

This is another northern specialty from Liguria, using a wonderfully complementary combination of tuna and anchovy with spinach and potatoes. Baked in a cake pan, it makes a good family dish—real Italian comfort food!

SERVES 4

12 oz russet or all-purpose potatoes

5 tablespoons olive oil, plus extra for brushing

fine dried bread crumbs for coating pan

2¼ lb spinach, tough stems removed

1 onion, peeled and minced

1 garlic clove, peeled and minced

handful of flat-leaf parsley, chopped

generous grating of nutmeg

2 eggs, plus 1 egg yolk

6 tablespoons freshly grated Parmesan cheese

4 oz canned tuna in best-quality olive oil

2 anchovy fillets, chopped

sea salt and freshly ground black pepper

1   Cook the potatoes in their skins in boiling salted water until soft, about 20 minutes. Drain and peel. Mash the potatoes smoothly, using a potato ricer or a food processor fitted with a fine grating disk, or by hand. Add 2 tablespoons of the olive oil to the potato purée and mix well.

2   Preheat the oven to 375°F. Line a 7-inch springform cake pan with parchment paper, then brush with a little olive oil. Sprinkle the bottom and sides with bread crumbs to coat, then carefully shake out any excess.

3   Wash the spinach well and place in a large pan with only the water that clings to the leaves after washing and 1 teaspoon salt. Cook over a medium high heat until wilted and tender. Drain thoroughly and, as soon as it is cool enough to handle, squeeze out as much moisture as possible using your hands. Chop the spinach coarsely.

4   Heat 3 tablespoons olive oil in a sauté pan, add the onion, and cook gently for 5 minutes. Add the garlic and parsley, then mix in the spinach and nutmeg, turning it over frequently. Add the contents of the pan to the potato purée.

5   Add the eggs, egg yolk, Parmesan, and some pepper, then flake the tuna into the mixture and add the anchovy fillets. Mix well, then taste and adjust the seasoning.

6   Spoon the tuna and potato mixture into the prepared pan and bake for 40 minutes. Serve warm or at room temperature.

stuffed braised squid

This is a specialty of Puglia. Cleaned whole squid are stuffed, then braised on a bed of vegetables and potatoes, for a rustic, comforting dish that looks so tempting. During cooking the potatoes take on the flavors of the fish juices to delicious effect. Use fresh rather than frozen fish, if possible.

SERVES 4–6

12 medium squid, 4–5 inches long, cleaned
  and tentacles reserved (see page 108)
3 tablespoons olive oil, plus extra for oiling dish
1 onion, peeled and sliced
1 garlic clove, unpeeled
2 large plum tomatoes, peeled, seeded, and
  coarsely chopped
1 tablespoon chopped flat-leaf parsley
1 lb russet or all-purpose potatoes
1 small, hot red chili pepper, seeded and
  chopped
6 1/2 tablespoons grated pecorino cheese
sea salt and freshly ground black pepper
flat-leaf parsley sprigs for garnish

FOR THE STUFFING:

5 oz (about 5 slices) dry, firm-textured bread,
  torn into small pieces
1 egg, lightly beaten
1 garlic clove, peeled and minced
1 tablespoon chopped flat-leaf parsley
finely grated zest of 1 lemon

1 First make the stuffing. Put the bread into a small bowl, add just enough warm water to cover, and let soak for 5 minutes. Drain and squeeze dry. Mix the bread with the rest of the stuffing ingredients, and season with salt and pepper.

2 Spoon the stuffing into the squid pouches, only half filling them to allow room for expansion during cooking. Seal the open end of the squid pouches with wooden toothpicks.

3 Preheat the oven to 350°F (unless you prefer to cook the dish on the stovetop). Lightly oil a 3-quart round casserole or Dutch oven. Scatter the onion, garlic, tomatoes, parsley, and 3 tablespoons water in the pot and season with salt and pepper.

4 Peel the potatoes and cut into 1/2-inch-thick slices. Arrange, slightly overlapping, on top of the onion and tomato mixture, and sprinkle with the chili and more salt and pepper. Arrange the stuffed squid pouches and tentacles on top. Sprinkle with the cheese and drizzle with 3 tablespoons olive oil.

5 Cover and cook in the oven for about 45 minutes, or simmer over a low heat on the stovetop for 1 hour,ß until the squid and potatoes are tender. Check the casserole occasionally to be sure it remains at a slow simmer. Garnish with parsley sprigs and serve.

6 poultry and meat

braised lemon chicken

A light, lemony-flavored chicken casserole, this needs nothing with it, apart from some crusty bread to mop up the juices and perhaps a leafy salad. You must use a good chicken though, or you could use chicken pieces—meaty thighs would be ideal.

SERVES 4

1 free-range chicken, about 3¹/₄ lb, cut
  into 8 pieces
2–3 tablespoons all-purpose flour for dusting
3 tablespoons olive oil

thinly pared zest of 3 lemons, minced
1 small onion, peeled and minced
2 sage sprigs, leaves only, chopped
1¹/₂ cups dry white wine
sea salt and freshly ground black pepper

1 Pat the chicken pieces dry with paper towels, then dust with flour to coat lightly all over.

2 Heat the olive oil in a large, heavy sauté pan over a medium high heat. Add the chicken pieces to the pan and brown well on all sides. Using a slotted spoon, transfer the chicken to a plate and season with salt and pepper to taste.

3 Reduce the heat to medium low and add the lemon zest, onion, and sage to the oil remaining in the pan. Sauté until the onion is golden and tender, about 10 minutes.

4 Return the chicken to the pan, along with the juices that have accumulated on the plate. Pour the wine over the chicken, partially cover the pan, and simmer gently for 50–55 minutes or until the chicken is very tender and most of the wine has evaporated. The chicken should be nutty brown in color and glazed with the pan juices. Check the seasoning.

5 Arrange the chicken pieces on warm plates. Skim the fat from the pan juices, then taste and adjust the seasoning. If too thick, stir in 1–2 tablespoons water. Pour the juices over the chicken and serve.

chicken with tomato and rosemary sauce

Known as *pollo in potacchio*, this dish has the aromas of the Marche region—garlic, chili, and lemon zest, allied with abundant rosemary. *Potacchio* describes a sauce that is added to chicken or rabbit for its final cooking. Just like any other herb, rosemary is sweeter in the spring with its new shoots, and gets stronger later in the year when you'll need to use it with discretion.

SERVES 4–6

1 free-range chicken, about 3¼ lb, cut
  into about 8 pieces

1 lemon, halved

2 tablespoons olive oil

4 tablespoons unsalted butter

⅔ cup dry white wine

1 onion, peeled and minced

1 garlic clove, peeled and minced

sea salt and freshly ground black pepper

FOR THE SAUCE:

3 shallots or 1 small onion, peeled

leaves from 2–3 rosemary sprigs

coarsely grated zest of 1 lemon

½ dried hot red chili pepper

3 tablespoons olive oil

14 oz canned crushed tomatoes

FOR GARNISH:

few small rosemary sprigs

1 Wash the chicken pieces and pat dry with paper towels. Rub them with the lemon halves, squeezing out the juice as you do so.

2 Heat the olive oil and butter in a large sauté pan. When the butter begins to foam, add the chicken pieces and fry on all sides until golden brown. Add the white wine, bring to a boil, and let bubble for 1 minute. Turn the heat down and add the onion. Cook for a few minutes to soften, then add the garlic and some salt and pepper. Cook for 20 minutes, turning the chicken from time to time.

3 While the chicken is cooking, prepare the sauce. Mince the shallots or onion, rosemary leaves, lemon zest, and chili together. Heat the olive oil in a frying pan and, when hot, add the minced ingredients. Sauté very gently for 5 minutes or so, then add the crushed tomatoes and some salt. Cook for 15 minutes, stirring frequently.

4 Now that the sauce is cooked, add it to the chicken, and stir to mix in the cooking juices at the bottom of the sauté pan. Leave over a gentle heat for 15 minutes longer, to allow the chicken to absorb the flavors of the sauce. Taste and adjust the seasoning, then serve scattered with rosemary.

chicken breasts with a vegetable relish

Chicken breasts are baked with onions and sage, then served with a Sicilian *caponata*-style relish—an eggplant stew with celery and yellow bell pepper that is slightly *agro dolce* (sweet and sour). You can vary the vegetables: mushrooms would be good inclusion.

SERVES 4

4 boneless chicken breast halves (with skin),
   each about 5 oz
1 tablespoon chopped sage
2 tablespoons olive oil
2 lb onions, peeled and very finely sliced
sea salt and freshly ground black pepper

FOR THE VEGETABLE RELISH:

$1\frac{1}{2}$ cups diced yellow bell pepper
$1\frac{1}{2}$ cups diced eggplant
1 cup diced celery
7 fl oz red wine vinegar
4 tablespoons olive oil
1 tablespoon tomato paste
1 tablespoon sugar

1 Preheat the oven to 400°F. Rub the chicken breasts all over with salt, pepper, and chopped sage. Use half of the olive oil to grease a small roasting pan or shallow baking dish.

2 For the relish, all the vegetables should be cut in $\frac{1}{2}$-inch dice. Put them into a saucepan with the wine vinegar and pour in 7 fl oz water; the liquid should be level with the vegetables. Add 1 teaspoon salt. Bring to a boil, then lower the heat and simmer for 10 minutes.

3 Meanwhile, lay the seasoned chicken breasts in the oiled pan or dish and scatter the onions on top. Sprinkle with salt, pepper, and the remaining olive oil. Bake for 20 minutes or until the chicken is tender and cooked through. To test, pierce the thickest part with the tip of a knife; the juices should run clear (not at all pink). The onion should be just tender, crisp on the top, and juicy underneath.

4 In the meantime, drain the relish vegetables. Heat the olive oil in a frying pan and stir in the tomato paste and sugar. Cook for 2 minutes, to caramelize the sugar. Now add the vegetables and turn to coat them in the caramelized sugar and oil mixture. Turn the heat down and cook for a further 15 minutes, stirring frequently. The vegetables should be just crisp. Season with salt and pepper.

5 Spoon the vegetable relish onto warm plates and top with the baked chicken breasts.

pheasant with olives

Pheasant is cooked during the Italian hunting season, which runs from September through to March. It is usually hung for a couple of days before cooking. Here, I have roasted the pheasant simply with olives, juniper berries, fennel seeds, and pancetta. This is how I imagine the *cacciatore*, or hunters, might cook their booty in their little stoves in the middle of the forest.

SERVES 2

1 pheasant
2 large slices pancetta or 4 bacon slices
1 cup pitted black olives
1 tablespoon fennel seeds
1 tablespoon unsalted butter
2 tablespoons olive oil
1 tablespoon juniper berries, crushed
1/2 cup dry white wine
1/4 cup chicken broth (page 47)
sea salt and freshly ground black pepper

1   Preheat the oven to 375°F. Place the pheasant on a board, wrap the pancetta or bacon slices around the breasts, and tie securely (they will help to keep the breast meat moist during roasting). Put the olives and fennel seeds into the pheasant cavity and secure with string.

2   Heat the butter and olive oil in a stovetop-to-oven casserole over a medium heat and brown the pheasant gently, turning frequently, for 20 minutes. Season with salt and pepper, and add the juniper berries. Pour in the wine and let it evaporate.

3   Add the chicken broth and place the casserole in the oven. Roast for about 30 minutes, basting frequently with the pan juices.

4   Cut the pheasant into serving pieces and arrange on a platter with the olives and fennel seeds. Place the casserole over a medium heat, add a little water or extra wine to deglaze, and scrape up the browned bits from the bottom, using a wooden spoon. Pour this sauce through a strainer over the pheasant and serve, with a salad or vegetables of your choice.

pancetta

Of the many wonderful Italian cured meats, pancetta is arguably the most useful in cooking and increasingly popular. It is the cured *pancia*, meaning paunch or belly of the pig—the Italian equivalent of our bacon, but much more flavorsome. You can also buy pancetta smoked, air-dried, and rolled with additional flavorings. It is sold by the piece or in slices, and also diced in convenient packs with an extended shelf life.

Pancetta is usually fried and used as a base for sauces, including the famous carbonara (see right). Sliced pancetta is excellent for wrapping over the breasts of birds to be roasted, or around vegetables to be baked. The fat enriches, moisturizes, and adds a wonderful flavor. Fried cubes are the most important element of a *soffritto*, a combination of vegetable dice and pancetta, used as the starting point for many great Italian dishes. The following recipes illustrate the versatility of pancetta; each serves 4.

▲ **pancetta and vegetable spiedini**
Cut 9 oz pancetta into fork-friendly pieces. Quarter 8 portobello mushrooms. Cut a large, peeled red onion into wedges. Cut a large zucchini into chunky rounds. Thread the pancetta, mushroom quarters, onion wedges, and zucchini chunks onto 4 skewers, interspersing with sage leaves. Cook under a preheated broiler, basting frequently with olive oil, for 10–15 minutes until the vegetables and pancetta are cooked.

pancetta-wrapped stuffed chicken breasts

You need 4 boneless chicken breast halves, each 5 oz. Cut a deep pocket horizontally in each one. Fill each pocket with a few baby spinach leaves, 1 tbsp cream cheese, and 2–3 sliced button mushrooms. Season well, then wrap each chicken breast in 2 slices of pancetta. Bake at 400°F for 20–25 minutes or until the pancetta is crisp and the chicken is cooked through. Serve with a green salad.

pancetta and tomato sauce (for pasta)

Fry 1 cup pancetta cubes in 1 tbsp olive oil until crisp. Add 2 crushed garlic cloves, a handful of chopped sage leaves, and 8 seeded and chopped plum tomatoes. Cook gently for 6 minutes. Toss with 11–12 oz freshly cooked pasta, such as bucatini or spaghetti. Serve scattered with 2 tbsp chopped flat-leaf parsley and lots of freshly grated Parmesan.

▲ spaghetti carbonara

Fry 1 cup diced pancetta with 1 minced garlic clove in 1 tbsp olive oil until crisp; let cool. Cook 11–12 oz spaghetti in the usual way. In a bowl, mix 2 very fresh eggs with 3/4 cup light cream and 2 tbsp freshly grated Parmesan, then add the pancetta with the pan juices. Drain the cooked spaghetti, return to the pan, and immediately pour in the carbonara sauce. Toss to coat, then let the egg "set" slightly. Serve with lots more grated Parmesan.

osso bucco con gremolata

This famous dish of stewed veal shanks originates from Lombardy. The pieces of veal are coated in seasoned flour, then braised in wine until meltingly tender. Here, they are served topped with my tangy version of the typical gremolata accompaniment.

Illustrated on previous page

SERVES 6

6 pieces of veal shank (osso bucco), cut about
  1¹/₂ inches thick
2–3 tablespoons all-purpose flour for dusting
2 tablespoons unsalted butter
¹/₂ cup dry white wine
finely pared zest and juice of 2 lemons
handful of flat-leaf parsley, minced
1 anchovy fillet in oil, drained and chopped
sea salt and freshly ground black pepper

1   Dredge the veal pieces in the flour, shaking off the excess. Melt the butter in a large, deep frying pan or sauté pan, then arrange the veal pieces in it. Brown over a medium heat, then turn carefully and brown the other side.

2   Pour in the wine and let it evaporate almost completely. Add some salt and pepper, cover tightly, and cook very gently for about 1¹/₂ hours, adding a little water from time to time to keep some liquid in the bottom of the pan.

3   Chop the lemon zest and mix with the parsley; set aside. Add the anchovy and lemon juice to the stew. Sprinkle the lemon and parsley mix over the top and serve immediately.

beef braised in Barolo wine

Piedmont is renowned for its fine aged Barolo, and this is a traditional, robust dish from the region. It's an excellent way of braising beef for a special occasion. If possible, use Barolo that is at least five years old, which will give a wonderfully thick, tasty sauce. Otherwise, a good bottle of a lesser full-bodied red wine will do.

SERVES 6

2$\frac{1}{4}$-lb boneless beef round roast, tied

2 carrots, peeled and chopped

1 medium onion, peeled and roughly chopped

2 celery stalks, roughly chopped

handful of flat-leaf parsley

3 bay leaves

1 tablespoon juniper berries

1 teaspoon black peppercorns

1$\frac{1}{2}$ cups aged Barolo wine, or other
   full-bodied red wine

1 tablespoon unsalted butter, in pieces

1 tablespoon olive oil

sea salt and freshly ground black pepper

1   Put the meat into a bowl and add the chopped vegetables, herbs, juniper berries, and peppercorns. Pour the wine over the meat, cover the bowl, and marinate in the fridge for at least 24 hours.

2   Preheat the oven to 350°F. Remove the meat from the bowl and dry well, reserving the marinade. Make little slits in the surface of the meat and insert the pieces of butter. Strain the marinade, saving the vegetables and flavorings, as well as the liquid.

3   Heat the olive oil in a stovetop-to-oven casserole. Add the meat and brown over a medium high heat on all sides.

4   Add the vegetables and flavorings to the meat. Add 1 cup of the reserved liquid and some salt. Cover and braise in the oven for about 3 hours, adding more of the reserved wine as needed to keep the meat from drying out.

5   When the meat is cooked, lift out and place on a warm platter; keep warm. Discard the bay leaves. Put the vegetables and other flavorings through a food mill with the cooking liquid (or blend in a food processor). Reheat this sauce, check the seasoning, and pour it over the meat to serve.

steaks with pizzaiola sauce

Pizzaiola sauce is so called because it features the typical pizza ingredients—olive oil, garlic, oregano, and tomatoes. It is always made with fresh tomatoes, cooked briefly until softened. This simple recipe is ideal for a special midweek supper, as it can be cooked very quickly when you return home from work.

SERVES 4

4 tablespoons olive oil

1 garlic clove, peeled

4 thin slices filet mignon, each about 5 oz

14 oz tomatoes, peeled, seeded, and
  coarsely chopped

1 tablespoon chopped oregano leaves, or
  2 teaspoons dried oregano

sea salt and freshly ground black pepper

FOR SERVING:
few radicchio leaves, shredded (optional)
handful of arugula leaves

1   Heat the olive oil with the garlic in a heavy-based frying pan over a high heat. Add the steak and brown quickly on both sides.

2   Add the tomatoes, season with salt and pepper, and turn down the heat. Sprinkle the oregano over the meat and tomatoes, partially cover the pan, and cook for 10 minutes.

3   Lift the tender pieces of meat from the pan and place on a warm plate; keep warm. Increase the heat and reduce the tomato sauce left in the pan by about half.

4   Serve the steaks on a bed of shredded radicchio if you like, surrounded by the tomato sauce. Scatter a few arugula leaves on top and serve at once.

lamb braised with fennel and tomatoes

Wild fennel grows prolifically in Sardinia, and the rugged terrain is sheep country, so this combination of lamb and fennel seems natural and almost inevitable. The flavors complement each other well, the fennel helping to cut the richness of the lamb.

SERVES 6

3 lb boneless shoulder of lamb
4 tablespoons olive oil
1 onion, peeled and chopped
2 cups canned peeled tomatoes
2 fennel bulbs, with fronds
sea salt and freshly ground black pepper

1 Trim the lamb of excess fat and cut into pieces about ³/₄ inch square. Heat the olive oil in a heavy casserole or Dutch oven, add the chopped onion and lamb pieces, and sauté over a medium high heat until the lamb cubes are browned all over.

2 Add the canned tomatoes to the casserole and season with salt and pepper. Cover and cook over a low heat for 10 minutes.

3 In the meantime, trim the fennel, reserving the feathery fronds, and cut into slices. Add the sliced fennel to the lamb and stir well. Cook, uncovered, for about an hour until the meat is tender, adding a little water from time to time to keep the meat moist, if necessary.

4 Taste and adjust the seasoning. Mince some of the reserved fennel fronds and scatter over the braised lamb and fennel to serve.

pot-roasted loin of pork

This is rather a grand dish, perfect for a dinner party. It's northern in influence, with Austrian touches like the juniper berries. The boned and rolled pork loin is pot-roasted in a sauce of wine, grappa, and sage until it is very tender, almost dropping off the bone.

SERVES 4–6

1 boneless center-cut pork loin roast, about
   3¹/₄ lb
1 celery stalk
1 onion, peeled
1 small carrot, peeled
1 garlic clove, peeled
6 sage leaves

3 rosemary sprigs
2 tablespoons olive oil
²/₃ cup dry white wine
3 tablespoons grappa (or vodka)
2 tablespoons juniper berries
1 cup vegetable broth (page 47)
sea salt and freshly ground pepper

1   Preheat the oven to 350°F. Season the pork loin all over with salt and pepper. Mince the celery, onion, carrot, garlic, sage, and leaves from 1 rosemary sprig.

2   Heat the olive oil in a stovetop-to-oven casserole, add the pork, and brown well on all sides. Lift the pork out and set aside on a large plate.

3   Add the chopped herbs, vegetables, garlic, and a little salt to the casserole and sauté for 5 minutes. Place the meat on top. Increase the heat, pour in the wine and grappa, and let bubble rapidly for a minute or so, turning the meat over once. Then add the juniper and half of the broth.

4   Cover the casserole and cook in the oven for 1¹/₂ hours or until tender, turning the meat twice and adding a little more broth if the vegetables appear too dry. To impart extra flavor, lay the other 2 rosemary sprigs on top of the pork about 15 minutes before the end of cooking.

5   To serve, carve the pork into slices. Strain the cooking juices and spoon them over and around the meat.

veal with pancetta and mushrooms

The rich, succulent flavor of this dish suggests that it has been cooking for hours, yet it is quick and easy to prepare for an after-work supper.

SERVES 4

1 cup diced pancetta

4 shallots, peeled and minced

6 medium cremini mushrooms, finely diced

1 tablespoon butter

6 tablespoons Marsala

handful of flat-leaf parsley, minced, plus
  extra for garnish

4 veal scallops, each about 4 oz

sea salt and freshly ground black pepper

1 Put the pancetta dice into a large, wide sauté pan or frying pan and cook over a medium heat until the fat begins to run and the pancetta is golden at the edges. Add the shallots and cook for about 5 minutes until translucent. Add the mushrooms with the butter and cook until tender.

2 Increase the heat slightly and add half the Marsala, scraping up the sediment from the bottom of the pan with a wooden spoon. Add the parsley and seasoning. Remove with a slotted spoon; set aside.

3 Return the pan to the heat. When it is hot, add the veal scallops with the remaining Marsala. Cook for 4 minutes on each side until tender and the liquid has evaporated. Serve topped with the pancetta and mushroom mixture, and scattered with a little chopped fresh parsley.

calf's liver Venetian style

Strips of calf's liver are fried very, very quickly in butter, and served with sweet onions braised in wine. This classic Venetian dish, known as *fegato alla veneziana*, is my mother's favorite.

SERVES 6

6 tablespoons unsalted butter

14 oz onions, peeled and thinly sliced

1/2 cup dry white wine

1 3/4 lb calf's liver, thinly sliced

sea salt and freshly ground black pepper

3 tablespoons chopped flat-leaf parsley
  for garnish

1 Heat half the butter in a frying pan, add the onions, and cook for 5 minutes or until golden. Add the wine and some salt and pepper. Cover and braise the onions over a low heat until very tender, about 25 minutes, stirring every now and again. Remove the onions and keep warm.

2 In the meantime, remove any gristle or membrane from the calf's liver, then cut into strips.

3 When the onions are almost ready, melt the rest of the butter in another frying pan. Add the liver and sauté over a high heat just until cooked through, about 4 minutes. Add salt to taste, then mix with the braised onions. Serve immediately, scattered with parsley.

marinated venison stewed in red wine

In the northern Alto-Adige region, chamois, or small deer, are hunted, cooked, and eaten during the shooting season. This special dish is typical of the region. The meat is marinated in full-bodied red wine with herbs before cooking, then served with a cream-enriched sauce made from the cooking liquid. Serve with "wet" polenta (page 96) and broiled mushrooms.

SERVES 6

3 lb boneless venison

4 tablespoons olive oil

2 tablespoons all-purpose flour

1/2 cup diced pancetta (preferably smoked)

1 onion, peeled and chopped

1/2 teaspoon ground cinnamon

1/2 teaspoon ground cloves

1 1/4 cups sour cream

sea salt and freshly ground black pepper

FOR THE MARINADE:

1 carrot, peeled and cut into pieces

1 large onion, peeled and coarsely sliced

1 celery stalk, cut into pieces

1 tablespoon coarse sea salt

2 tablespoons juniper berries, crushed

8 black peppercorns, bruised

3 whole cloves

1 rosemary sprig

3 tablespoons olive oil

3 bay leaves

3 garlic cloves, peeled

1 bottle Barolo or other full-bodied red wine

1 Put all the ingredients for the marinade into a large bowl. Cut the venison into 2-inch pieces and add to the marinade. Stir well, then cover and let marinate in the refrigerator for about 12 hours.

2 Using a slotted spoon, lift the meat from the marinade, drain, and pat dry with paper towels. Strain the marinade and reserve. Preheat the oven to 375°F.

3 Heat 2 tablespoons olive oil in a large, heavy-based frying pan. Working in batches, brown the meat all over, then transfer to a side plate. Add the flour to the pan and cook until brown, stirring and scraping up the sediment on the bottom of the pan. Gradually stir in about half of the strained marinade and bring to a boil, stirring constantly.

4 Heat the remaining 2 tablespoons olive oil in a large stovetop-to-oven casserole and fry the pancetta for 5 minutes. Add the onion with a pinch of salt and cook until it is soft.

5 Now add the meat with its juices, the wine sauce from the frying pan, and about 2/3 cup of the remaining marinade. Season with salt and pepper, and add the ground spices. Bring slowly to a boil, then cover the casserole and place in the oven. Cook for 1 hour, adding a little more of the marinade twice during the cooking.

6 Add the sour cream to the casserole. Return to the oven and cook for a further 30 minutes or longer, until the meat is very tender. The cooking time will depend on the age of the animal.

7 vegetables and salads

baked onions with prosciutto and Parmesan

A delicious, rib-sticking winter dish from Lombardy, this can be prepared in advance ready to pop into the oven. The onions are stuffed with bread crumbs flavored with plenty of prosciutto and Parmesan, then baked until sweet and tender. Serve as an antipasto in the winter, or as a vegetable side dish.

SERVES 4 or 8

8 large white onions, peeled
2 tablespoons coarse white bread crumbs
1/2 tablespoon milk
5 oz prosciutto, minced (about 2/3 cup)
6 tablespoons freshly grated Parmesan cheese
1 egg, beaten
1 tablespoon unsalted butter, in pieces, plus
  extra to grease
sea salt and freshly ground black pepper

1 Add the onions to a pan of boiling salted water and simmer for 15 minutes. Meanwhile, soak the bread crumbs in the milk. Preheat the oven to 350°F.

2 Drain the onions, reserving the liquid. Rinse under cold running water, then drain and pat dry with paper towels. Cut a thin slice from the top of each onion and scoop out the centers, using a teaspoon; keep half of the onion flesh that you remove. Place the onion shells upside down on a board while you prepare the filling.

3 Mince the reserved onion. Squeeze the bread crumbs to remove excess liquid and place in a bowl with the minced onion. Add the prosciutto, Parmesan, and beaten egg. Season with salt and pepper, and mix well. Spoon the stuffing into the onion shells.

4 Grease a baking dish with butter and arrange the onions in it. Dot with butter and moisten the onions with 4 tablespoons of the reserved cooking liquid. Bake for 40 minutes, basting the onions from time to time with the pan juices. Serve hot.

cabbage leaves stuffed with leeks and mushrooms

Stuffed vegetables are commonplace in Italy, and most recipes come from around Rome. Here, though, the aspect is more northern, in that cabbage is used. These attractive little bundles can be assembled ahead of time, and the filling can be as varied as you like—try mozzarella and anchovies, for instance.

SERVES 4

1 head Savoy cabbage

2 tablespoons unsalted butter

2 garlic cloves, peeled and minced

8 oz leeks, washed, trimmed, and minced

4 oz cremini mushrooms, wiped and minced

6 tablespoons slivered almonds

2–3 teaspoons lemon juice

2 teaspoons paprika

1 egg, beaten

2/3 cup vegetable broth (page 47)

sea salt and freshly ground black pepper

1 Preheat the oven to 400°F. Select 8 large, darker, outer leaves from the cabbage. Blanch these leaves in boiling salted water, or steam, for 1–2 minutes to soften slightly. Drain, then cut away the tough center stems.

2 Mince enough of the remaining cabbage to give 2 cups. Melt the butter in a large frying pan. Add the garlic, leeks, mushrooms, and minced cabbage, and fry gently, stirring frequently, for 10 minutes.

3 Add the almonds, lemon juice, and paprika to the leek mixture and cook over a low heat for 5 minutes. Remove from the heat and let cool. Add the beaten egg and some salt and pepper to the cooled stuffing and mix well.

4 Divide the stuffing among the blanched cabbage leaves and roll up tightly, tucking in the sides as you roll. Pack the cabbage rolls into a baking dish, placing them join-side down. Pour the vegetable broth around them and cover the dish with foil. Bake for 20 minutes. Serve hot.

Roman artichokes

Artichokes grow all over Italy, but the Lazio region, and Rome in particular, is especially renowned for its small, tender artichokes. Specialty dishes feature on restaurant menus throughout the capital during the artichoke season. Try to buy young artichokes with long stems, as these are tender and won't yet have developed much in the way of a choke. For this appetizer the artichokes are best served warm.

Illustrated on previous page

SERVES 4

4 medium globe artichokes
I lemon, cut in half
3 bay leaves
²/₃ cup dry white wine
FOR THE DRESSING:
large handful of mint leaves
2 garlic cloves, peeled
3–4 tablespoons extra virgin olive oil
2 tablespoons white wine vinegar
sea salt and freshly ground black pepper

1 Prepare the artichokes one at a time. Trim the base of the stem at an angle, then peel the stem. Cut off the leaves about ¼ inch from the top. Rub the cut surfaces with a lemon half. Now start peeling away the artichoke leaves, removing at least four layers, until the leaves begin to look pale. Spread open the top leaves and reach down with a teaspoon to scrape out the choke. Immerse the artichoke in a bowl of cold water with the other lemon half added (to prevent discoloration). Repeat to prepare the rest of the artichokes.

2 Place the bay leaves, lemon halves, wine, and artichokes in a large pan and add enough cold water to cover. (The artichokes should fit snugly in the pan.) Bring to a boil, cover, and simmer for about 30–35 minutes until the artichokes are tender. Drain thoroughly.

3 To make the dressing, mince the mint leaves with the garlic, then place in a bowl with the olive oil, wine vinegar, and salt and pepper to taste. Whisk to blend thoroughly.

4 Arrange the artichokes upside down (with their stems sticking up) on serving plates. While still warm, pour the dressing over them and serve.

creamy potato casserole with prosciutto

This is very similar to the French *gratin dauphinoise*, and it's ideal served after (or with) a simple meat dish. A little minced garlic can be added to increase the flavor, or, for a more subtle taste, rub a cut garlic clove around the dish with the butter. The casserole can be prepared and baked ahead, then reheated to serve.

SERVES 6

2¹/₄ lb russet or all-purpose potatoes

2 tablespoons unsalted butter

4 oz prosciutto slices

2 cups milk

1 cup light cream

2¹/₄ cups freshly grated Parmesan cheese

freshly grated nutmeg, to taste

sea salt and freshly ground black pepper

1   Preheat the oven to 350°F. Peel the potatoes and slice them thinly. Grease a large, shallow baking dish with half of the butter. Lay the potato slices in the dish, overlapping them slightly. Lay the slices of prosciutto on top.

2   In a bowl, mix together the milk, cream, and half of the grated Parmesan, and season with nutmeg, salt, and pepper. Pour the mixture over the potatoes. Sprinkle with the remaining Parmesan and dot with the rest of the butter.

3   Bake until the potatoes are tender, about 45 minutes. If necessary, increase the oven temperature toward the end of the baking time to brown the crust. Serve hot.

Neapolitan vegetable casserole

Known locally as *ciambotta*, this is Naples' answer to ratatouille. It's an easy dish, and one that can be cooked ahead of time. Vary the vegetables as you like—perhaps adding celery or fennel.

SERVES 4

1 medium eggplant
1 medium onion, peeled
1 red bell pepper
2 medium potatoes, peeled
1 zucchini, trimmed
3 tablespoons olive oil
1 garlic clove, peeled and crushed
2–3 teaspoons fennel seeds, crushed
14 oz canned peeled plum tomatoes
6 tablespoons red wine
2 teaspoons dried oregano
sea salt and freshly ground black pepper

1   Cut the eggplant into cubes. Sprinkle with salt, place in a colander, cover with a plate, and weight down with a can of food. Leave to drain out the bitter juices for 15 minutes.

2   Meanwhile, chop the onion. Halve, core, and seed the red pepper. Cut the red pepper, potatoes, and zucchini into similar sized chunks. Rinse the eggplant cubes and pat dry.

3   Heat the olive oil in a saucepan, add the onion, and cook gently for about 5 minutes or until softened, then add the garlic and cook for a minute. Add all the vegetables and remaining ingredients. Bring to a simmer and cook gently for 25–30 minutes until the vegetables are tender, adding a little water to moisten during cooking if necessary. Serve hot.

peas with green onions and pancetta

Freshly shelled young green peas are cooked quickly with sauteéd green onions and chopped salty Italian bacon in one pan. This is how Italians appreciate the sweet flavor of our most popular vegetable.

Illustrated right

SERVES 4–6

2 tablespoons olive oil

2 bunches of green onions, trimmed and
   roughly chopped

1 cup diced pancetta

$3^1/_2$ cups shelled fresh or frozen green peas
   (preferably fresh)

handful of flat-leaf parsley, chopped, plus a
   sprig for garnish

sea salt and freshly ground black pepper

1   Heat the olive oil in a large frying pan over a medium heat. Add the green onions and pancetta, and sauté until the onions are translucent.

2   Add the peas, salt, pepper, and $^1/_2$ cup boiling water. Bring to a simmer and cook, uncovered, until the peas are tender, about 5–7 minutes for fresh peas, 3–4 minutes for frozen ones.

3   Drain off any excess water, then add the chopped parsley and toss together. Transfer to a warm bowl and top with the parsley sprig.

braised fennel with pecorino

Fennel is sautéed in butter and olive oil until tender, then served topped with pecorino cheese shavings. This tempting dish is especially good after fish.

SERVES 4

2 fennel bulbs, with fronds

2 tablespoons unsalted butter

1 tablespoon olive oil

5 oz pecorino cheese, pared into shavings

sea salt and freshly ground black pepper

1   Trim the fennel bulbs, reserving a few of the feathery fronds for garnish. Cut each fennel bulb in half from top to bottom. Blanch in boiling salted water for 5 minutes, then drain.

2   Melt the butter with the olive oil in a heavy-based sauté pan or frying pan over a medium heat. Add the halved fennel bulbs and cook for 10–12 minutes or until tender and golden brown, turning from time to time to color evenly. Season with salt and pepper.

3   Transfer to a warm serving plate and scatter with pecorino shavings. Garnish with the fennel fronds and serve at once.

salad leaves and dressings

Italians love their salads. They are regarded as a digestive, a healthy way to settle the stomach, so a side salad often follows the main course. Typically this is a selection of salad leaves with a simple dressing of good extra virgin olive oil and lemon juice or vinegar, plus seasoning.

Many fine salad leaves originate from Italy, including peppery arugula, lollo rosso, lollo biondo, and radicchio. Often the shape and texture of the leaves dictates the style of dressing: sturdier leaves can take a thicker dressing. Only use very fresh salad leaves. Wash them just before preparing the salad, then drain and carefully pat dry with paper towels.

Of course, other ingredients can be added to salads for texture and flavor, including cooked vegetables such as eggplants, artichoke hearts, and fennel, tomatoes and other fruits, freshly chopped herbs, olives, anchovies, capers, pine nuts, sun-dried tomatoes, and small pieces of bread.

▲ all-purpose Italian dressing

This is my all-time favorite dressing, which I use to dress bitter leaves, such as curly endive and arugula, as well as crisp romaine leaves. In a bowl, mix the juice and finely grated zest of 1 lemon, a crushed 1/2 garlic clove, 4 tbsp extra virgin olive oil, salt, and pepper. Whisk to combine. Add about 1 tbsp freshly grated Parmesan cheese, which immediately makes the dressing thicker and creamier. Blitz in a blender or food processor for a smoother dressing. Use at once.

basic balsamic vinaigrette

You can use this vinaigrette to dress meats and vegetables, as well as salad leaves. In a bowl, mix 2 tbsp good, aged balsamic vinegar with 1/2 cup extra virgin olive oil, or a combination of olive and sunflower or other oil of your choice. Season with salt and pepper, and whisk well. Balsamic jelly (sold in a jar) can be used instead of the vinegar; dilute it to taste with oil, to make your dressing as thick as you like.

anchovy-based dressing

Use this to dress arugula, spinach, radicchio, and any other member of the endive family. Gently heat 1/2 cup fruity extra virgin olive oil in a small pan, then add a minced shallot and sweat until soft. Add 6 chopped anchovies, 3/4 cup dry white wine, a minced garlic clove, and a handful of torn basil leaves. Gently warm through, then blitz in a blender or food processor until smooth. Pass through a fine strainer and season to taste (but go easy with the salt).

▲ Sicilian salad

A refreshing salad dressed with fruity olive oil. To prepare, peel and slice 6 oranges (blood oranges when in season) into thin rounds. Trim and slice a medium fennel bulb; save a few feathery fronds. Combine the fennel and oranges, snipped fennel fronds, and 3 tbsp chopped fresh walnuts. Dress with 2 tbsp extra virgin olive oil, season with salt and pepper, and let stand for an hour or so, turning occasionally. Serve with a few romaine leaves.

marinated zucchini

This is a typical southern recipe from Campania. Finely sliced zucchini are oven-dried, then fried and marinated in wine vinegar and fruity olive oil with freshly chopped mint. For optimum flavor, marinate the zucchini overnight.

SERVES 6

9 large zucchini, trimmed

3/4 cup olive oil

FOR THE DRESSING:
large handful of mint leaves, coarsely chopped
3 garlic cloves, peeled and minced
6 tablespoons white wine vinegar
4 tablespoons extra virgin olive oil
sea salt

1 Preheat the oven to 275°F, and line two large baking sheets with parchment paper.

2 Cut the zucchini lengthwise into thin slices and place in a single layer on the lined sheets. Leave in the oven for about an hour to dry out completely without coloring.

3 Heat the olive oil in a large frying pan and fry the zucchini in batches until golden; there's no need to turn them. Drain carefully on paper towels.

4 Transfer the zucchini slices to a serving bowl and sprinkle with the chopped mint and garlic. Drizzle the wine vinegar and extra virgin olive oil over the zucchini, and season with salt to taste. Cover and let stand for 2 hours or, better still, overnight.

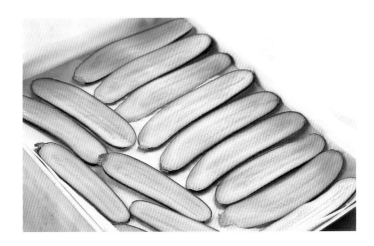

caponata

The secret of this classic *agro dolce* (sweet-sour) Sicilian dish is to cook the eggplants separately and combine them with the tomato sauce at the last moment, so their individual flavor is retained. Flavored with olives, capers, and pine nuts, the caponata can be served hot or cold, as an antipasto or vegetable dish. It will keep well in the refrigerator for several days.

SERVES 4

2 medium eggplants
4 tablespoons olive oil
1 onion, peeled and sliced
14 oz canned crushed tomatoes, drained
3 celery stalks, trimmed
1 tablespoon capers, rinsed
$^1/_3$ cup pitted green olives, rinsed
4 tablespoons white wine vinegar
1 tablespoon sugar
2 tablespoons pine nuts
handful of flat-leaf parsley, chopped
sea salt and freshly ground black pepper

1 Cut the eggplants into 1-inch cubes. Sprinkle with salt, place in a colander, cover with a plate, and weight down with a can of food. Leave to drain out the bitter juices for 15 minutes, then rinse to remove the salt and pat dry with paper towels.

2 Heat 3 tablespoons of the olive oil in a large frying pan. Add the eggplant cubes and fry, turning, until brown and tender. Drain on paper towels, and keep to one side.

3 Heat the remaining 1 tablespoon olive oil in a saucepan, add the onion, and fry for 5 minutes until golden. Add the tomatoes and some salt and pepper, and simmer for 15 minutes.

4 Meanwhile, cut the celery into $^1/_2$-inch pieces. Add to the tomato sauce along with the capers, olives, vinegar, and sugar. Simmer for 15 minutes longer until reduced slightly, stirring occasionally.

5 Put the eggplant and pine nuts into a serving dish and pour the tomato sauce over them. Stir, then let stand for at least 30 minutes. Scatter with the chopped parsley just before serving.

Tuscan cabbage and cannellini beans on toast

This dish can be served as a first course or antipasto, or as a vegetable. The contrast of the black cabbage and white cannellini beans makes it visually appealing. Dress the whole thing with new season's extra virgin olive oil to bring out all the flavors. If you haven't time to cook dried beans, use a 14-oz can cannellini beans instead; drain, rinse, and flavor with a little crushed garlic and chopped thyme.

SERVES 6

1 cup dried white cannellini beans,
* soaked in cold water overnight*
2 rosemary sprigs
3 bay leaves
3 thyme sprigs
3 flat-leaf parsley sprigs
4 garlic cloves, unpeeled
1 lb cavolo nero (or green cabbage),
* stems removed*
6 slightly dry slices of fine-textured, country-style
* bread*
extra virgin olive oil for drizzling
sea salt and freshly ground black pepper

1   Drain the cannellini beans and place in a large pan. Add plenty of cold water to cover, along with the herbs and 3 unpeeled garlic cloves. Bring to a boil, then reduce the heat and cook for about 1½ hours or until the beans are tender.

2   Preheat the oven to 400°F. Roughly chop the cavolo nero leaves and add to a pan of boiling salted water. Return to a boil and simmer for 10–15 minutes until tender.

3   Arrange the bread slices in a single layer on a baking sheet and bake for 3 minutes. Turn them over and bake for a further 3 minutes. In the meantime, peel and halve the remaining garlic clove. While the bread is hot, rub one side with the garlic.

4   Drain the beans and discard the herbs and garlic. Arrange the bread on a plate, garlic side up. Scoop the cavolo nero from the pan using a slotted spoon, drain well, and arrange on the bread slices. Spoon the hot cannellini beans on top. Drizzle with extra virgin olive oil, season with salt and pepper, and serve immediately.

8 desserts and sweets

meringues with chocolate sauce

Classic Italian meringue has a wonderful silky texture, but it does involve boiling sugar syrup and the use of a candy thermometer, so I have opted for the easier alternative here. This simple method produces meringues that are crisp on the outside. Put pairs together with cream and serve with a luxurious chocolate sauce.

SERVES 4

3 egg whites

3/4 cup + 2 tablespoons superfine sugar

1 cup heavy cream

FOR THE CHOCOLATE SAUCE:

7 oz (7 squares) bittersweet chocolate, broken
    into pieces

1/2 cup milk

1 Preheat the oven to its lowest setting. Line a large baking sheet with parchment paper.

2 Whisk the egg whites in a clean bowl until stiff and glossy. With patience, add the sugar very gradually, whisking well between each addition. The meringue should be stiff and shiny.

3 Spoon the meringue into a pastry bag fitted with a 1-inch plain tube and pipe about 16 mounds, each about 2 inches in diameter, on the baking sheet, spacing them well apart.

4 Dry out the meringues in the oven for about 2 hours until crisp, but still white. Peel the meringues away from the paper and place on a wire rack. Let cool completely.

5 For the sauce, melt the chocolate with the milk in a heatproof bowl set over a pan of gently simmering water. Remove from the heat and stir until smooth. Cool slightly, or completely if you prefer to serve the sauce at room temperature.

6 To assemble, whip the cream until it holds soft peaks. Put pairs of meringues together with the cream, then arrange on a serving dish. Pour the chocolate sauce over the meringues and serve.

caramelized fruit salad with zabaglione sauce

Fresh seasonal fruits—especially peaches, nectarines, cherries, and pears—are often served at the end of a meal in Italy. As an alternative, I sometimes serve a medley of fruits under a caramelized zabaglione topping. The result is delicious, and not dissimilar to a fruit crème brûlée. Either use a large, shallow baking dish or individual gratin dishes.

SERVES 4

1 cup strawberries, hulled

1 kiwi fruit

1 pear

1 cup raspberries

2 tablespoons Vin Santo (or
   1 tablespoon Marsala)

FOR THE ZABAGLIONE:

3 egg yolks

6 tablespoons superfine sugar

2$^{1}/_{2}$ tablespoons Marsala

TO FINISH:

1–2 teaspoons confectioners' sugar, sifted

1 Halve or slice the strawberries. Peel and slice the kiwi fruit. Peel, core, and slice the pear. Leave the raspberries whole. Combine the fruit in a baking dish (or individual gratin dishes) and sprinkle with the Vin Santo or Marsala.

2 To make the zabaglione, put the egg yolks and sugar into a heatproof bowl and whisk until creamy and almost white in color. Gradually add the Marsala, whisking constantly until the mixture is well combined.

3 Set the bowl over a saucepan of simmering water and cook over a medium heat, beating constantly with the whisk, until the zabaglione is creamy and thick.

4 Pour the hot zabaglione over the fruit. Sprinkle with the confectioners' sugar. Place under a preheated broiler for 30 seconds, or wave a blow-torch over the surface, until the zabaglione begins to brown. Serve immediately, with vanilla ice cream if desired.

baked stuffed peaches

The Mediterranean climate is ideal for growing peaches, and Italian peaches, in particular, are prized for their juicy, fragrant flesh. This recipe is a classic from Lombardy. Halved peaches are stuffed with a mixture of ground almonds, crumbled amaretti, and cocoa powder, then drizzled with dry white wine and baked until tender.

Illustrated on previous page

SERVES 4

4 large, ripe peaches

9 amaretti cookies, crushed

1/4 cup ground almonds

1 egg yolk

1 tablespoon unsweetened cocoa powder, sifted

1 1/4 cups dry white wine

2 tablespoons brown sugar

1 Preheat the oven to 350°F. Wash the peaches and pat dry. Cut them in half following the natural line and remove the pit. Using a teaspoon, scoop out a little of the pulp from the middle of each peach half to create a cavity. Mince the scooped-out pulp.

2 In a bowl, combine the minced peach pulp, crushed amaretti cookies, ground almonds, egg yolk, and cocoa powder, and mix thoroughly until evenly blended. (Alternatively, blend in a food processor for a few seconds until smooth.)

3 Fill the peach cavities with the almond mixture and place side by side in a baking dish. Pour the wine over the peaches, sprinkle with the brown sugar, and bake for 25 minutes.

4 Let the peaches cool and serve at room temperature, drizzled with the cooking juices.

coffee zabaglione

Zabaglione is the most famous classic Italian dessert, made from egg yolks, sugar, and Marsala—the vital flavoring ingredient. Over the years, new ways of serving zabaglione have evolved (see page 172), and you come across different flavor variations in Italy. Here I have added espresso coffee for a delicious twist. Serve the zabaglione warm, with seasonal fruit if you like, or freeze it to make a wonderful ice cream with a soft texture, rather than ice hard. Note that this recipe uses lightly cooked egg yolks (see note on page 5).

SERVES 4

4 egg yolks
2 tablespoons superfine sugar
pinch of Italian "00" flour or cake flour
2 tablespoons freshly made espresso coffee
1 teaspoon whole milk
¼ cup dry Marsala

1 Combine the egg yolks, sugar, and flour in a large heatproof bowl and set over a pan of gently simmering water, making sure the base of the bowl is not in direct contact with the water. Beat constantly, using a balloon whisk. As the sugar dissolves, the mixture will become runny, then as it cooks the zabaglione thickens to the consistency of heavy cream. This takes about 5 minutes.

2 At this point, pour in the espresso, milk, and Marsala. Continue to beat with the balloon whisk until the zabaglione becomes thick and fluffy. This should take about 5 minutes.

3 Remove the bowl from the pan and let the zabaglione rest for 10 minutes. Spoon into glasses and serve warm.

4 Alternatively, cool and freeze in a shallow container, covered, for 3 hours. Whisk, then freeze again for 2 hours or until firm. Serve scooped into glasses.

ricotta cheesecake with strawberry sauce

This baked cheesecake has a superb texture and flavor, which is partly due to the ricotta—Italy's light, versatile soft cheese. The accompanying strawberry purée adds a sweet, refreshing note. You could also fold some chopped nuts or raisins into the ricotta filling, if desired.

SERVES 6

FOR THE PASTRY:
2¹⁄₂ cups Italian "00" flour, plus extra for dusting
¹⁄₄ cup sugar
¹⁄₂ cup (1 stick) unsalted butter, softened
1 egg, plus 1 egg yolk
¹⁄₂ teaspoon vanilla extract
finely grated zest of 1 small lemon
¹⁄₂ teaspoon baking powder

FOR THE FILLING:
2 eggs, separated
²⁄₃ cup sugar
4 tablespoons unsalted butter, softened
finely grated zest of 1 lemon
1 teaspoon vanilla extract
1¹⁄₄ cups ricotta cheese
1 teaspoon thin honey
1 teaspoon baking powder

FOR THE SAUCE:
1 cup strawberries, hulled
juice of 1 lemon
1 tablespoon sugar

1 To make the pastry, combine all the ingredients in a food processor and process until the mixture is evenly blended and comes together as a ball of dough. If the pastry is a little too sticky, add a bit more flour. Wrap the dough in plastic wrap and let rest in the refrigerator for about 30 minutes.

2 Preheat the oven to 300°F. Roll out the pastry on a lightly floured surface to ¹⁄₈ inch thick. Use to line an 8-inch springform cake pan, or a deep, loose-based tart pan, pressing the pastry onto the bottom and up the sides. Set aside.

3 For the filling, beat the egg yolks, sugar, butter, lemon zest, and vanilla together with an electric mixer until smooth. Add the ricotta, honey, and baking powder, and mix gently until evenly blended. In a separate bowl, beat the egg whites until they hold firm peaks, then gently fold into the filling.

4 Pour the filling into the pastry shell and bake for 2¹⁄₂ hours. Let cool in the pan on a wire rack. Chill until ready to serve.

5 For the sauce, purée the strawberries, lemon juice, and sugar in a blender, then pass through a strainer into a bowl. Cover and chill for 30 minutes.

6 Carefully unmold the cheesecake onto a flat plate. Serve in slices, topped with a small ladleful of strawberry sauce.

almond pudding with bitter chocolate sauce

This is a very old recipe, dating back to the Middle Ages. Almonds were introduced into Sicily by the Arabs during their occupation of southern Italy and they feature in this pudding. A dark chocolate sauce complements the flavor well.

SERVES 4

1¹/₃ *cups blanched almonds*

grated zest of 1 lemon

2 teaspoons unflavored gelatin granules

13 fl oz milk

²/₃ *cup sugar*

1 teaspoon vanilla extract

1 tablespoon Grand Marnier

4 oz (4 squares) bittersweet chocolate, finely
   chopped

1   Put the blanched almonds into a blender or food processor and grind to a fine paste. Transfer to a bowl and stir in ³/₄ cup warm water and the lemon zest. Mix thoroughly and set aside to rest for 1 hour. Strain the almond liquid into a bowl.

2   Sprinkle the gelatin over 1 tablespoon cold water in a bowl and let soften for 5 minutes. Pour ²/₃ cup of the milk into a saucepan and add the sugar and vanilla extract. Slowly bring to a boil over a low heat, stirring to dissolve the sugar. Add the gelatin and whisk briefly to dissolve.

3   Remove from the heat and add the almond liquid, Grand Marnier, and remaining milk. Mix well, then pour into a 10-inch ring mold and refrigerate for 3 hours.

4   Melt the chocolate in a bowl set over a pan of hot water. Stir until melted and very smooth. Remove the bowl from the pan and let cool slightly.

5   Briefly dip the mold into hot water, then unmold the pudding onto a serving plate. Drizzle some of the melted chocolate sauce on top; pass the rest separately.

my grandmother's espresso pudding

This very simple dessert, which is rather like a coffee crème caramel, has been in my family for generations, and my grandmother often made it. She was very frugal, and would always use leftover coffee in ice creams, baked puddings, and cakes.

SERVES 4

2 cups brewed espresso coffee, cooled

³/₄ cup sugar

5 eggs, beaten

1 teaspoon lemon juice

1¹/₂ cups heavy cream

1   Combine the cooled espresso and half the sugar in a large bowl and stir well. Add the beaten eggs, a little at a time, mixing thoroughly. Set aside.

2   Put the remaining sugar, the lemon juice, and 1 tablespoon water into a small, heavy-based pan. Cook over a medium to high heat until the mixture turns a pale caramel color. Immediately pour the caramel into a shallow 10-inch ring mold or 1-quart shallow, round baking dish, tilting it in all directions to distribute the caramel over the bottom and sides. Continue to tilt until the caramel has hardened. Let cool for 30 minutes.

3   Preheat the oven to 350°F. Pour the coffee mixture into the caramel-lined mold and place in a large roasting pan containing enough water to come halfway up the sides of the mold. Bake for 1 hour until the pudding is set and a wooden toothpick inserted in the center comes out dry. Let the pudding cool for 1 hour.

4   To serve, unmold onto a serving plate. Whip the cream until thick and pile into the center (if you have used a ring mold), or serve individual portions with a dollop of whipped cream.

apple cake

This light Genoese sponge layered with apples is delicious with coffee for breakfast, or for an afternoon snack. To vary the flavor, try adding a little minced fresh rosemary to the batter.

SERVES 6–8

1–2 teaspoons vegetable oil
1–2 tablespoons dried bread crumbs
1/2 cup (1 stick)) unsalted butter
1 lb Golden Delicious apples
4 eggs
3/4 cup granulated sugar

1 1/4 cups Italian "00" flour
1 teaspoon baking powder
pinch of salt
6 tablespoons milk
finely grated zest of 2 lemons
confectioners' sugar, sifted, for dusting
rosemary sprigs to finish (optional)

1 Preheat the oven to 350°F. Brush the inside of a 9-inch cake pan with the oil, then sprinkle with the bread crumbs and shake off the excess. Melt the butter and set aside to cool. Peel, quarter, and core the apples, then slice thinly.

2 Put the eggs and granulated sugar into a heatproof bowl set over a pan of gently simmering water. Beat for 10–15 minutes until the mixture is thick and pale, and leaves a trail on the surface when the beaters are lifted out. Remove the bowl from the heat and continue beating until the mixture is cool.

3 Sift the flour with the baking powder and salt. Fold half of this mixture gently into the beaten eggs and sugar. Slowly trickle the melted butter around the edge of the bowl and fold it in gently. Take care to avoid knocking out the air and losing volume. Fold in the remaining flour mixture, then the milk and lemon zest, and finally the apple slices.

4 Pour the batter into the prepared pan. Bake for 45 minutes or until a skewer inserted in the center comes out clean. Leave in the pan for 5 minutes, then unmold onto a wire rack and let cool. To serve, dust the top of the cake liberally with confectioners' sugar and scatter with rosemary sprigs, if desired.

cheeses

Italy produces many superb cheeses. Aged, hard Parmesan and creamy blue Gorgonzola are famous the world over; other excellent varieties include pecorino (made from sheep's milk), mozzarella (from buffalo milk), and soft, creamy ricotta.

Cheese is used a great deal in cooking, but it is also eaten as a course on its own, often instead of a dessert. Typically a generous wedge of one excellent cheese is served with fruit, such as grapes, apples, or pears, or nuts, or a crisp salad vegetable. Of course, you can serve a selection of cheeses, if you prefer.

In the south we finish a meal with a local cheese plus some celery or fennel, or fresh nuts. An unusual Italian custom is to serve a sharp cheese topped with fruit or nuts and drizzled with a little honey. This is eaten with a knife and fork. Pecorino, honey, and walnuts is a classic combination; the contrast of saltiness and sweetness is wonderful.

▲ pecorino and fennel salad
To serve 4, thinly slice 2 small fennel bulbs, and shave 14 oz pecorino romano cheese into wafer-thin slices, using a swivel vegetable peeler. Arrange the cheese, fennel, and a handful of arugula leaves on 4 plates. Scatter a small handful of toasted pine nuts on top. Drizzle with 3 tbsp extra virgin olive oil and sprinkle with black pepper and a little sea salt.

Sardinian cheese crackers

Make these to serve with cheese. Mound 1¼ cups Italian "00" flour on a work surface and make a well in the middle. Add a medium egg, ¾ cup grated pecorino cheese, and a pinch of salt. Mix together, adding enough water (about 4 tbsp) to make a soft dough. Break into small pieces and roll into balls, then flatten to very thin disks. Deep-fry in hot olive oil for about 5–6 minutes until golden. Drain well.

Italian cheese and balsamic jelly

Balsamic jelly is one of my recent discoveries. Sold in jars, it is available from some specialist food markets. It tastes wonderful and is the ideal complement to full-flavored Italian cheeses, such as Gorgonzola or a sharp pecorino. Serve a wedge of either cheese with a generous spoonful of balsamic jelly, plus some grapes or pear, if desired.

▲ Gorgonzola, pear, and toasted walnuts

To serve 4, toast 12 fresh walnuts in the oven at 400°F for 5–7 minutes; don't let them burn. Peel and core 4 pears, then cut into thin wedges. Arrange the pear wedges on 4 plates, and crumble 4 oz Gorgonzola cheese over them. Top with the toasted walnuts and drizzle with some fragrant thin honey.

chocolate-coated figs with almond stuffing

Figs are plentiful in Italy, and this dried fruit delicacy, *fichi mandorlati*, comes from the Calabria region. The attractive chocolate-dipped figs make an ideal foodie gift, especially at Christmas. For best results, use good-quality dried figs, and massage them lightly with your fingers to plump them up before stuffing.

MAKES 12

12 whole blanched almonds
finely pared zest of 3 oranges
12 dried figs, preferably Italian
8 oz (8 squares) bittersweet chocolate

1   Preheat the broiler. Spread the almonds on a foil-lined baking sheet and toast under the broiler, about 5 or 6 inches from the heat, until golden. Turn them frequently and watch carefully to make sure they don't burn. Let cool.

2   Mince the orange zest and scatter on a board. Slit the figs vertically and place an almond inside each one. Roll the figs in the orange zest to coat all over.

3   Meanwhile, break the chocolate into pieces and put in a heatproof bowl set over a saucepan of simmering water. Leave until melted, then remove from the heat and stir until smooth.

4   One at a time, spear the figs with a fork and partially dip in the chocolate, turning to coat all around. Place on a sheet of parchment paper and let dry and set.

chocolate "salami"

This sweetmeat comes from Emilia-Romagna, where the cooks are incredibly creative. It's a combination of chocolate, nuts, cookies, and brandy, which is rolled into a sausage, chilled until set, and then sliced. You can make the rolls as fat or thin as you like, but never huge because the mixture is very rich! Smaller disks make ideal petits fours. Serve with coffee.

SERVES 4–6

$2/3$ cup raisins

8 oz (8 squares) bittersweet chocolate

4 tablespoons unsalted butter

$1/4$ cup sugar

$3/4$ cup coarsely chopped blanched almonds

8 oz plain, buttery cookies, such as shortbread,
  coarsely crushed (about $2^{1/4}$ cups)

1 tablespoon brandy

$1/3$ cup coarsely chopped mixed candied peel

1 egg yolk

1 Soak the raisins in warm water to cover for about 15 minutes until plump, then drain and set aside.

2 Break the chocolate into pieces and place in a large heatproof bowl with the butter. Set over a saucepan of gently simmering water until melted. Remove the bowl from the pan and stir until smooth.

3 Add the sugar, almonds, cookies, raisins, brandy, and candied peel to the melted chocolate and mix well. Return the bowl to the pan and stir in the egg yolk until evenly incorporated. Remove from the heat and let the mixture cool completely.

4 Turn the mixture onto a sheet of parchment paper and shape into a roll with your hands. Wrap the chocolate "salami" in the paper and twist the ends to seal. Refrigerate for several hours to firm up. To serve, remove the paper, cut the salami into thin slices, and arrange on a serving plate.

almond biscotti

Almonds are used as a basis for these crisp cookies from Prato in Tuscany, which are traditionally served with Vin Santo. Their Italian name, *biscotti*, comes from the French "*bis cuit,*" meaning "twice baked." You can vary the recipe if you like, using hazelnuts instead of the almonds, or adding some chopped chocolate.

SERVES 4–6

2¼ *cups Italian "00" flour*

¾ *cup + 2 tablespoons sugar*

1½ *teaspoons baking powder*

½ *teaspoon salt*

2 *eggs, plus 1 egg yolk*

1 *cup roughly chopped blanched almonds*

1 Preheat the oven to 350°F. Mix the flour, sugar, baking powder, and salt together in a bowl. Add the eggs and egg yolk, and mix well to form a smooth dough. Knead in the chopped almonds.

2 Divide the dough into 4 portions and form each into a cigar-shaped log. Place the logs on a floured baking sheet, spacing them well apart. Bake for about 20 minutes, until golden brown.

3 Cut the logs into ½-inch slices while still warm. Separate them and lay flat on the baking sheet. Bake for 15 minutes longer.

4 Transfer the biscotti to a wire rack to cool. Store in an airtight container until required.

index

Acknowledgments

Firstly, I dedicate this book to Mark Salter, who loved life and food in equal measures. Secondly, I should like to thank all those who have helped to make this such a special book: Jane O'Shea for her guidance, Janet Illsley, for her total professionalism, Peter Cassidy for his truly outstanding photography, Linda Tubby for making the food look so wonderful, and Vanessa Courtier for art direction and design. I am also very grateful to Susan Fleming for working with me again and putting me in order, and to Katie O'Donnell for her speed and patience. You are all such fun to work with. Last, but not least, I thank Richard Moore, my husband, for his terrific advice and support.